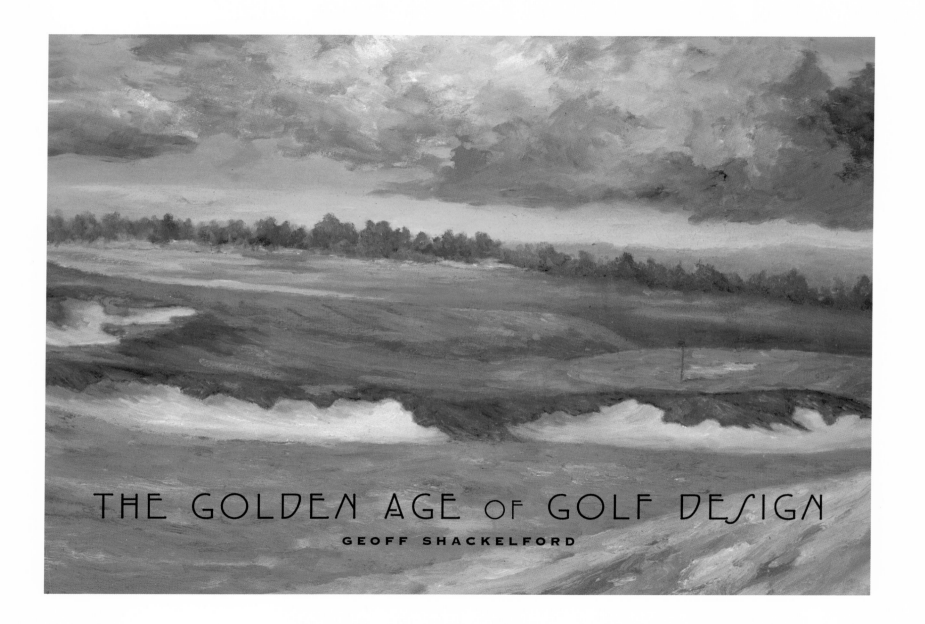

THE GOLDEN AGE of GOLF DESIGN

GEOFF SHACKELFORD

Sleeping Bear Press
121 South Main Street
P.O. Box 20
Chelsea, MI 48118
www.sleepingbearpress.com

Printed and bound in Canada.

10 9 8 7 6 5 4 3 2 1

Library of Congress Cataloging-in-Publication Data
Shackelford, Geoff.
The golden age of golf design / by Geoff Shackelford.
p. cm.
ISBN 1-886947-31-7
1. Golf courses-United States-Design and construction-History-20th century.
2. Golf course architects-History-20th century. I. Title
GV975.S521999
796.352'06'8-dc21   98-32093
                    CIP

TABLE of CONTENTS

ACKNOWLEDGEMENTS

Many graciously offered their sage advice and support during the creation of this book, and I apologize in advance for anyone I might have left out, for it surely was not intentional. As always, Ben Crenshaw, Geoffrey Cornish, Brian Lewis, my parents Lynn and Diane, my grandparents Ray, Louise and Etta, and many other friends and family supported the book and efforts to get it in print. I can't thank Mike Miller enough for creating such original paintings that bring the classic courses back to life. His work has opened my eyes to the parallels between golf architecture and other kinds of artistic creations. Architects Ron Forse, Gil Hanse, Tim Liddy, Bruce Hepner, Tom Doak, Don Placek, Mike DeVries, Bill Coore, Ross Forbes, Michael Hurdzan, Dave Axland, Dan Proctor and others provided their thoughts and information with regard to the master architects. At the various clubs, several historians and members were most helpful in securing photographs and information: Rick Wolffe, Bob Trebus and Stuart Wolffe at Baltusrol; Jim Marshall at Pine Valley; Bill Kittleman at Merion; Neal Hotelling at Pebble Beach; Jim Langley at Cypress Point; David Chag at The Country Club; Pete Smith at Shinnecock Hills; Doug Petersan at Baltimore Country Club; John Robinson at St. George's Hill.

Eternal gratitude goes to Saundra Sheffer and Marge Dewey at the Ralph W. Miller Golf Library. If it weren't for this thorough collection and these wonderful ladies and all of their support, this book would never have happened. At Golf House, Patty Moran and Maxine Vigliotta were extremely helpful and I can't thank you enough for your patience and kindness. Also, fellow golf writers George Bahto, Bradley Klein, Daniel Wexler, Gib Papazian,

Sid Matthew, David Outerbridge and the late Pete Jones provided plenty of information and were always helpful in answering questions.

My thanks to the many others who provided guidance, photos or leads. In no particular order: Vince Monahan, Tom Gray, Connie Lagerman, Geoff Curtis, Michael Stern, Alex Galvan, Wade Horracks, Nancy Battet, Mike Riste, Dorothy Brown, Bob Beck, Reg Dwight, Karen Bednarski, Terry Buchen, Karen Hewson, Jim Frank, Carolyn Cole, Doug Brooks, George Brown, Gordon Sumner, Bill Zmistowski, John Fleming, Tom Langford, David Goddard, The Thomas Family, James Dodson, Eric Shortz, Pete Smith, John Anderson, Nick Leefe, Barclay Douglas, Bob Sessman, John Keough, Joe Pantaleo, Ray Haddock, the Hagley Museum staff, the USGA and the Tufts Archives.

The book would never come together or looked as lovely as it does without the diligence of those at Sleeping Bear Press: Jennifer Lundahl who created a beautiful design; Lynne Johnson and Lara Vaive who guided it through production from beginning to end; Danny Freels, who edited the text so assiduously; and everyone else who contributed to its completion—thank you.

Finally, my most sincere gratitude goes to all of the men and women who documented the Golden Age and who worked to make it such an important time in the history of golf. The Golden Age architects left us with so many masterpieces to cherish. I hope this book serves as a tribute to their designs and to the hard work of those who built their masterful courses and whose names we'll never know. I hope this book will remind us how fortunate we are to have had such talented artists designing and building courses during the early years of the twentieth century.

INTRODUCTION

An example of early geometric design, circa 1900. This is the original Annandale Golf Club in Pasadena, California. Note the oiled sand green and chocolate drop mounds.

At some point in their life every adult longs for the "good old days" when things were simpler and times were better. Sometimes, in our desire to paint the past as an idyllic time, we selectively ignore certain facts that might taint our rosy remembrances of the way things used to be. Sometimes our nostalgia for times past is justified, other times it is not. For the game of golf, there was no better or more prosperous time than the 1920s. The twenties really were the good old days.

Many will argue that the 1940s and early 1950s, when Nelson, Hogan and Snead ruled the game, was golf's Golden Age. However, beginning in 1911, when Charles Blair Macdonald opened The National Golf Links of America on Long Island, golf took an important step forward and did not look back until the leanest years of the Great Depression. Not only were virtually all of the greatest courses in America built during this twenty-five year period, the game itself expanded rapidly thanks in large part to the inspiring play of Bobby Jones.

In the early 1890s, you could count the number of golfers in the United States on two hands. By 1930 there were 2.25 million Americans playing the game. The number of golf courses had

"Viewing the monstrosities created on many modern golf courses which are a travesty on Nature, no golfer can but shudder for the soul of golf. It would seem that in this striving after 'novelty and innovation,' many builders of golf courses believe they are elevating the game. But what a sad contemplation! Motoring to Southampton, I pass a goodly number of new courses. As I view the putting greens it appears to me they are all built similarly, more or less of a bowl or saucer type, then built up toward the back of the green, and then scalloped with an irregular line of low, waving mounds or hillocks, the putting green for all the world resembling a pie-faced woman with a marcel wave. I do not believe any one ever saw in nature anything approaching these home-made putting greens. Then scattered over the side of the fairway are mounds modeled after haycocks or chocolate drops. The very soul of golf shrieks!"

— *C.B. Macdonald*

increased from 742 in 1916 to a total of 5,691 by 1930. The people of the United States were putting World War I behind them by creating better transportation, using new modes of communication and enjoying fresh forms of recreation.

Aided by rapid economic expansion, the decade between 1920 and 1930 was perhaps the most creative, daring and innovative period in American history. In no place was this more evident than in golf course architecture, where early layouts were transformed from mundane and geometrically-edged mediocrities, to grand-scaled, artistic and strategically designed masterpieces.

Sadly, golf course architecture has never come close to scaling the heights it achieved between 1911 (when C. B. Macdonald opened his ideal course on Long Island) and 1937 (when Perry Maxwell constructed the first nine holes at Prairie Dunes). A look at any of the rankings in contemporary golf magazines reveals that an overwhelming majority of the top courses were created during this Golden Age. Recently, *Golfweek* magazine resorted to splitting their rankings into two eras, operating on the valid premise that it is not possible to compare more recent design work with the classics of the past.

So how did this happen? What made the Golden Age such a special time, and why hasn't anything since measured up to the superiority of this era?

For one thing, the Great Depression and World War II played significant and understandable roles in squelching the desire of American architects to try something more bold and daring than the Golden Age work. In addition, American golfers have drastically changed their expectations for golf architecture and the game's style of play from the way it was played in the 1920s. Today, beauty and stroke play are in; strategy and match play seem to be a thing of the past.

The primary inspiration back then was still the Scottish way of playing shots close to the ground. And match play, which allowed architects more freedom to create daring holes where high scores might be racked up from time to time, had not been overtaken by stroke play as the primary method of competition. Also, luck was considered an interesting facet of the game during the Golden Age, whereas in today's game architects and superintendents are asked to do everything in their power to eliminate luck, which certainly limits the more creative design concepts.

The modern American game is also plagued by

a mechanical, numbers-driven mind-set. If a layout does not stretch to well over 7,000 yards and play to a par 70 or more, it is not considered a worthy test of golf. If the course record is low and the layout is vulnerable to good scores, there must be something faulty in its design. Of course, nothing could be further from the truth. Great courses yield to skillful golf and joy can be found on any well-designed course, no matter what the scorecard says.

Today's courses are rarely designed to make golfers think. More often than not, they seem to only serve as beautiful settings in which golfers may launch shots high into the air only to land on soft, green turf. However, the primary mark of a top course during the Golden Age was not its prettiness or the color of its grass, though the Golden Age designers certainly created the most stunning bunkers and contours ever seen. But the landmark courses from the Golden Age were special then and timeless now because of their ability to test the mental as well as the physical component of the golfer's game, a concept better known as strategy.

The Golden Age came about because of many unique factors falling into place most conveniently. Time brought on a negative reaction to

Chocolate drop mounds on the College Arms Golf Club course in Deland, Florida, circa 1910.

4

Departure from Geometric Design, Sketch by Walter Travis

One of the first architects in the United States, Travis was a prominent player and editor of The American Golfer. *He had a major influence on early golf architecture. Travis wrote on the subject from time to time and gave examples of what golfers should be looking for, as he did with this pair of sketches. On the left is what Travis referred to as the "Old Style of Bunkers" and on the right was the more strategic "Modern System of Traps." Besides the shift from penal design, note the change in styles where the bunkers are irregularly shaped and fairway and green edges are less geometric.*

the many early geometric designs, and architects soon began studying the classic links of Great Britain and adapting the principles of the best holes into their work. The early designers were also not afraid to collaborate and share information for the betterment of the game. Travel became more convenient and construction methods improved. Finally, several prominent writers started talking about the courses and even a few of the early professionals wrote about principles embodying the finest layouts.

By no means are these factors the only contributors to the Golden Age, but each played a major role in defining the courses and the character of the master architects.

Reaction to Geometric Designs
The earliest American golf courses were simply dreadful. Somehow, the charm and naturalness of the old links of the British Isles was lost when

the game made its way across the Atlantic, resulting in virtually no designs of architectural significance during the late 19th and early 20th century.

Many of the first American courses were primitive and sometimes downright freakish, with their dead flat oil greens, chocolate drop mounds and grave-shaped hazards. Even Shinnecock Hills on Long Island, one of the five founding members of the United States Golf Association (USGA) and one of the very best American courses today, once had unnaturally square bunkers prior to its brilliant redesign by William Flynn in 1930.

Though C.B. Macdonald's 1911 opening of The National Golf Links ushered in the Golden Age, Herbert Leeds' Myopia Hunt Club design in Massachusetts and Devereux Emmet's redesign at Garden City Golf Club in New York actually preceded Macdonald and were the first evidence that primitive architecture was headed out the door. It was their example, along with an influx of English and Scottish superintendents and golf pros like Donald Ross, that led to a greater understanding of the game and a negative reaction to the early and primitive American designs.

Not Afraid to Study and Adapt

Each prominent architect of the Golden Age either studied the finest courses of the British Isles or learned about their more interesting characteristics and incorporated the best elements from those layouts into their work. C.B. Macdonald was the first to state openly that he was imitating the principles of the great holes, and many architects followed suit.

By no means did they build actual replica holes. Instead, the architects were incorporating ideas that had worked well in Britain and they were showing American golfers "the possibilities." Most were careful to explain that this was merely the beginning, and that fresh ideas and innovations would come along later as the art of design matured. Though practicing architects from the later years of the Golden Age did become more innovative, the Depression put an end to the careers of many inventive architects and the profession has suffered from a lack of artistic depth ever since.

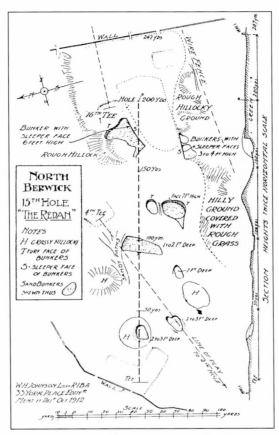

Survey of the original Redan hole at North Berwick in Scotland, the most imitated hole in all of golf.

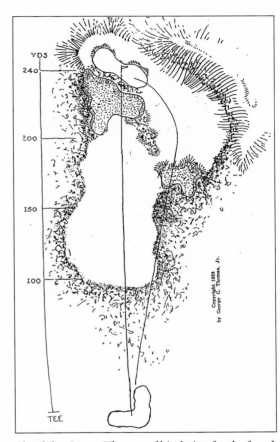

Sketch by George Thomas of his design for the fourth hole at Riviera Country Club in Pacific Palisades, California. Note how he uses the principles and bunkering placement of the Redan, but alters many of its original features to adapt to the site in question and the prescribed length of the Riviera version.

5

6

George Thomas explains his ideas to Dr. Alister MacKenzie during construction of Riviera.
MacKenzie was paying a visit on his way through Los Angeles. The Golden Age architects frequently visited each other's designs in progress to offer advice.

Collaboration

Throughout the Golden Age, amateur and professional architects were not afraid to consult with one another. Despite some colossal egos, men like C.B. Macdonald knew that the future of the game in America depended on high-quality golf courses. Thus, the sharing of opinions was commonplace.

This was also a time when Americans respected those who had ideas and convictions. They expected and looked forward to a lively discussion and a good argument. They were not threatened by those with differing views. Instead, they loved the opportunity to have an intellectual debate for the good of the subject at hand, whether it was art, music, politics or golf architecture.

George Crump conducted tours for anyone who visited his Pine Valley site in New Jersey. And even though no one really knows how many opinions Crump actually heeded, the finest course in America was created. It's hard to imagine that Pine Valley would be the course it is today had Crump not consulted so many brilliant minds.

Bobby Jones hits tee shots in the dirt at the eighth hole at Augusta National while Dr. Alister MacKenzie and other club officials look on.

7

Travel by train not only became commonplace, it became a popular social activity.

Easier Travel and New Construction Techniques

When demand for more golf courses grew in the suburbs and the western United States, the ease of train travel made it possible for top architects to make a living designing courses. Donald Ross made the most use of trains. Often he would travel to a site, spend a day or two routing the course and then leave the construction up to a crew, never to return to see the results of his ideas.

The types of equipment employed by architects changed dramatically during the Golden Age. The early part of the era saw the widespread use of horse-drawn slip scrapers and man's hand. During the late 1920s, steam shovels and road scrapers began to be used in the construction of golf courses, and by the early 1930s bulldozers were employed regularly. Not only did these advances improve the quality of layouts being built, it allowed for golf courses to be built faster and with more dramatic features. Also, better methods of drainage and tree removal made it possible to build on inland sites once considered unsuitable for golf.

Innovative ways to eliminate trees and other obstacles paved the way for architects to build courses on inland terrain during the Golden Age. This sequence shows how trees that had been cut down were disposed of at St. George's Hill, an H.S. Colt masterpiece in Britain.

9

Crews prepare the St. George's Hill ground after tree stumps have been detonated (see previous page photo). The painstaking process is a reminder just how difficult inland courses were to construct during the Golden Age.

Bernard Darwin
Darwin created the art of golf course commentary, among many other things.

"I take it that the difficulty to which the humble golfer does object is that which comes from ever increasing length of holes. If ever there is a revolution of the golfing proletariat it will be on account of sheer length and not of fierce bunkers."
— *Bernard Darwin*

Horace Hutchinson
One of the first early figures in golf to write about course construction, maintenance and design.

The Written Word

Several authors and players began writing about golf courses in the early 1900s and their words influenced the architects of the Golden Age. Two-time British Amateur Champion John Low was the pioneer with his 1903 book, *Concerning Golf.* It contained one of the earliest essays ever written on the subject of golf course strategy and design. Low wrote other letters and articles detailing his thoughts, and years later everyone from Alister MacKenzie to C.B. Macdonald referred to his words.

Horace Hutchinson, who authored in 1886 what many believe is the first instruction book on golf, was also one of the first to write about the principles of design and was cited by many Golden Age architects as a major influence, particularly in the field of golf course maintenance.

Bernard Darwin may have been the most influential of all golf writers. Not only was he as prolific a golf essayist as the game has ever seen, but his original style, critical commentary and descriptive passages about the courses of the British Isles made golfers take a serious look at the layouts they were playing. His 1910 *The Golf Courses of the British Isles*, illustrated in conjunction with the gentle watercolors of artist Harry Rowntree, was the first book devoted solely to golf courses and their features. Darwin's book, along with many of his essays, stand today as a monumental work in the vast literature of golf.

John L. Low

John Low was one of the most important early figures in golf and a major influence on Golden Age golf architects. Here is a sampling of his influential writings on architecture.

"The true hazard should draw the play towards it, should invite the golfer to come as near as he dare to the fire without burning his fingers. The man who can afford to take risks is the man who should gain the advantage."

"Bunkers, if they be good bunkers, and bunkers of strong character, refuse to be disregarded and insist on asserting themselves; they do not mind being avoided, but they decline to be ignored."

"No game depends so much as golf on its arena for success: on an interesting course an interesting game will be played; on a badly planned green the game will be dull."

"The trick of the thing is to make the ground dictate the play. The shot from the teeing ground is nearly always far too wide: it is a case of driving anywhere straight ahead. The good architect will see to it that the hole proclaims that you must keep well to the left, or well the right, as the case may be. And so in each stroke in the round there should be some special interest which demands some special maneuver."

"Every fresh hole we play should teach us some new possibility of using our strokes and suggest to us a further step in the progress of our golfing knowledge."

I n this book, each chapter features a particular "school" of design. Needless to say, there were no actual schools and to this day, there is no official educational program for those hoping to become golf architects.

Each Golden Age "school" holds a prominent place in the history of course design, and several traits appear consistently throughout the various schools. Each was highly creative and distinctive in style. Each was influenced by the Old Course at St. Andrews in Scotland and its overseer, Old Tom Morris. And, sadly, each school has since seen drastic changes to the design integrity of its courses that often make many of their masterpieces unrecognizable.

The purpose of this book is to celebrate the various schools and to look at the Golden Age courses before the Great Depression, World War II, and other elements forced many clubs to cut back on maintenance costs by filling in bunkers or, in some cases, abandoning their layouts altogether during the difficult times. *The Golden Age of Golf Design* will also demonstrate how superior many of these courses were before club green committees and greenkeepers found out how inexpensive specimen trees really were, and turned some of these artistic masterpieces into arboretums!

Some "schools" are not as well represented photographically as others simply because certain architects were not as concerned with documentation as others. While the focus here is on American design work, it should be noted that some of the finest courses ever built were also constructed abroad during the same period, including MacKenzie's many fine designs in Australia with Alex Russell and others, H.S. Colt's work in the British Isles, and Tom Simpson's designs throughout Europe.

However, this book is mainly about the most important and creative time in North American golf course architecture — The Golden Age of Golf Design.

CHAPTER ONE

THE EARLY INFLUENCES

"The more I studied the Old Course, the more I loved it and the more I loved it, the more I studied it."

— *Bobby Jones*

The most creative period in golf course design was inspired in large part by just two sources: the Old Course at St. Andrews and its most noted caretaker, Old Tom Morris. Naturally there were other influences, such as the old links at Prestwick and North Berwick in Scotland, and eventually, early architects like Herbert Fowler and H.S. Colt.

However, it is St. Andrews and its timeless charm that awakened many architects to the possibilities of course design. The Old Course is strategic golf at its finest. Every hole provides numerous options of play, and the best route to the hole is dictated by the varying conditions and the location of the flagstick.

The beauty of St. Andrews is that it plays differently every day and requires the golfer to adapt to its ever-changing strategy. No golf course in the world requires more thought and skill, yet the player who plans his attack and executes it successfully can do very well on the Old Course. Much of the St. Andrew's charm lies in its quirkiness and evolution. It has been refined and modernized over the years, first by Allan Robertson, and later by the townspeople and St. Andrews' longtime administrator, pro and greenkeeper, Old Tom Morris.

Old Tom nurtured the course and refined it into today's masterpiece. It was also Old Tom who introduced many of its subtleties to future architects such as C.B. Macdonald, Alister MacKenzie, A.W. Tillinghast and Donald Ross. They, in turn, incorporated numerous elements of the Old Course into their work. There is a little bit of the Old Course's strategy and nuance in every golf course, especially in the best designs of the Golden Age. The first full-time architect to leave a lasting impression on the game was H.S. Colt, who would later introduce C.H. Alison and Alister MacKenzie to the profession. Colt was also instrumental in the early planning stages of Pine Valley Golf Club, perhaps the benchmark design of the Golden Age.

In the United States, there were several other important early sources. Though none were as important as Old Tom and the Old Course, men like Herbert Leeds, Walter Travis and the creators of Pennsylvania's Oakmont Country Club, Henry and William Fownes, all played a role in influencing golf course design.

OLD TOM MORRIS

At the age of 30, Old Tom Morris was the pro at one of Scotland's most important early courses, Prestwick Golf Club, where he eventually won three of his four Open Championships. He had apprenticed under Allan Robertson at St. Andrews before moving over to Prestwick. He had mastered the art of golf club and ball manufacturing and was in demand as a pro and greenkeeper. In 1867, Old Tom returned to St. Andrews as its pro and over the next twenty years would teach many young men how to play golf. He also further developed the arts of ball and club manufacturing, greenkeeping and golf course design.

Having established himself as the first-ever golf architect, Old Tom received requests from many towns and clubs to consult on the creation of a golf course or the renovation of their existing layout. One of those courses was Dornoch, in the northernmost part of Scotland. A few years later, Old Tom would tutor one of Dornoch's finest young players, Donald Ross. Other future architects who visited Old Tom were C.B. Macdonald, Alister MacKenzie and A.W. Tillinghast.

Old Tom created the basic routings and design of Muirfield, Prestwick, Royal Dornoch and Royal County Down. He redesigned the Old Course at St. Andrews, Carnoustie and Machrihanish, all landmarks in Scotland. Not bad for someone who regarded his design work as a hobby and whose design fee was one pound.

"Old Tom is the most remote point to which we can carry back our genealogical inquiries into the golfing style, so that we may virtually accept him as the common golfing ancestor who has stamped the features of his style most distinctly on his descendants."

— *Horace Hutchinson*

Photograph by A.W. Tillinghast, 1898.
"As I recall, the photograph of Old Tom was taken during the summer of 1898. It had been my great privilege to know the rare old man quite well. He then was about seventy-seven years of age or thereabouts, for he was in his eighty-seventh year when he died from a fall ten years later. I met him first some thirty-four years ago and although I never saw him again after 1901, he did write me several brief notes. At the time when the photograph was taken we had been chatting in his shop and I happened to have with me my "Lattern" as Andra Kirkaldy used to call my camera. Old Tom was not at all inclined to pose for photographs but I cajoled him to the open shop door. This fortunate likeness was the result, for he declared it was the best ever made of him. Aside from any merit as a photograph, I do know it was very like him, for his true, kindly nature shows straight from his eyes. The picture shows him looking out over the Home Green, which he told me had been built over the bones of dead men, and where he still held the flag for the finish of all important matches."

— *A.W. Tillinghast*

A Typical St. Andrews Sod Wall Bunker.
"St. Andrews has the most perfect golfing hazards which the mind can imagine, but even there these traps are not always successful in catching the bad shots; for the course contains too much good ground outside of the bunkers."

— *John Low*

17

The "Hell" Bunker on the Old Course at St. Andrews.
"I believe the real reason St. Andrews' Old Course is infinitely superior to anything else is owing to the fact that it was constructed when no-one knew anything about the subject at all, and since then it has been considered too sacred to be touched. What a pity it is that the natural advantages of many seaside courses have been neutralized by bad designing and construction work."

— *Alister MacKenzie*

The Home Hole at St. Andrews during the 1920s.
"Nowhere in the world is golf so little cut and dried. It is a course of constant risks and constant opportunities of recovering, of infinitely varied and, to the stranger, unorthodox shots."

— *Bernard Darwin*

"Providence has been very kind in dowering St. Andrews with plateau greens, and they are never easy to approach. A plateau usually demands of the golfer that a shot should be played; it will not allow him merely to toss his ball into the air with a lofting iron and the modest ambition that it may come down somewhere on the green."

— *Bernard Darwin*

18

HERBERT FOWLER

(1856-1941)

Described by Bernard Darwin as one of "the most gifted architects" of his time, Herbert Fowler was a quick thinker who often insulted clients because of his swift judgments about the potential of their course. Fowler's first design effort may have been his finest, the Old Course at Walton Heath. He spent two years between 1902 and 1904 building the Surrey, England course for friends of his wealthy father who had commissioned him because of Herbert's successful amateur golf career.

Fowler's triumphant design at Walton Heath led to more work in the British Isles, especially with many new course properties popping up in the expanding Heathlands region. His redesign work at Royal North Devon and Royal Lytham and St. Anne's drew more praise, and Fowler soon branched out to the United States. Joining his design firm at the time was the eccentric Tom Simpson, who would later write one of the finest books on golf course design and construction and a landmark publication during the Golden Age, *The Architectural Side of Golf.* Simpson focused on the firm's work in the British Isles while Fowler traveled overseas to America. Herbert Fowler's most noted work in the United States was at Eastward Ho! in Massachusetts and a 1921 redesign of Los Angeles Country Club, while his best work with Simpson was their 1926 creation in Scotland, Cruden Bay.

Even though he didn't agree with Fowler's style of architecture, Alister MacKenzie praised Fowler for modernizing American golf and for setting "a standard which other architects attempted to emulate."

19

HARRY S. COLT

(1869-1951)

A Cambridge graduate and practicing lawyer for a number of years, H.S. Colt was also a fine player who became so interested in golf architecture that he dropped his law work altogether and became a full-time architect. His first design was in London during the early 1900s, with many other pre-World War projects following soon after.

Colt's workload became so heavy that he added several fine associates. The first was his lifelong partner in design, C.H. Alison. Colt also formed a brief partnership with Alister MacKenzie whom Colt met while working at MacKenzie's home course, Alwoodley in England. Colt was perhaps the first prolific, full-time golf course designer in England, and he set the standard for other professional architects of the Golden Age. He presented attractive renderings, wrote articles on the subject, penned *Golf Course Architecture* with C.H. Alison in 1920, and was the first to create golf course tree planting schemes. Colt's tree plans were presumably to forestall any future plantings by club committees.

The list of H.S. Colt's important design and redesign work is filled with landmark courses. Though his work in the United States with Alison was limited and ranges from brilliant to uninspired, his consulting work at Pine Valley was invaluable. Colt spent a week with George Crump and helped with the routing of the holes and consulted on other matters. His design with C.H. Alison at Timber Point Golf Club on Long Island was celebrated upon its opening as being part Pine Valley and part National Golf Links, with vast areas of sand, marsh and the bay coming into play on several holes.

In the British Isles, Colt redesigned and created the modern versions of Sunningdale and Wentworth, England's two most noted inland courses. He was responsible for what many consider to be the most sound example of architecture in all of Scotland—Muirfield.

H.S. Colt was a master at routing courses and was a brilliant strategist. His ideas influenced many successful Golden Age designers, particularly his one-time friend and associate Alister MacKenzie. His portfolio of courses, his writings, and the subsequent work of those he trained, confirm H.S. Colt's significance in the history of golf architecture.

20

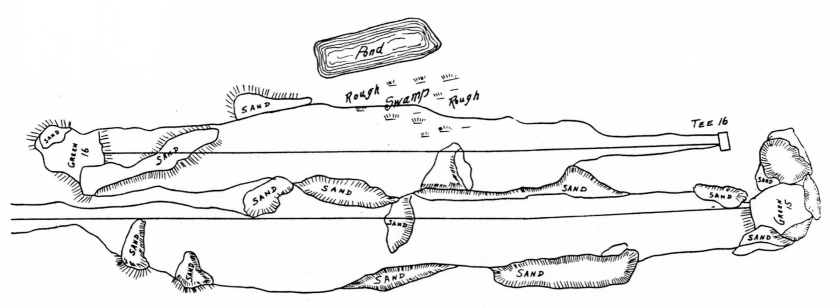

Colt Drawing of Parallel Hole Design for Indian Hill, in Winnetka, Illinois.
Colt was the first architect to tackle difficult properties and always considered speed of play in his design work.

"An architect's earnest hope is, without doubt, that his courses will have the necessary vitality to resist possibly adverse criticism, and will endure as a lasting record of his craft and of his love for his work."

— *H.S. Colt*

Eighth Hole, St. George's Hill, Surrey, England, Par-3, 175 Yards
Famous one-shotter designed by H.S. Colt. Notice the attractive bunkering style, which was emulated by many American architects during the Golden Age.

"Hazards should be visible. In general, they should not penalize to the extent of more than one stroke, provided that the stroke out of them is properly played. They should not be so severe as to discourage bold play. In placing hazards it is vital to keep the course navigable for the duffer. It is perfectly possible to do this, and yet to render it interesting and testing for the first-class player."

— *C.H. Alison*

Fifth Hole, Sunningdale Golf Club—New Course, Par-3
H.S. Colt's work at Sunningdale in 1921-22 led to the creation of the New Course and the redesign of the existing Old Course. Colt's design and bunker style was a major influence on the many architects who practiced in the United States, and the firm of Colt and Alison was involved in many prominent early projects in the U.S., most notably Pine Valley.

CHARLEſ HUGH ALIſON (1882-1952)

The often-forgotten member of H.S. Colt's architecture firm, C.H. Alison was a prolific designer for many years, particularly in the Far East where he spent a significant amount of time. A fine player and member of the Oxford and Cambridge Golfing Society, Alison met Colt while Colt constructed a new course at Stoke Poges in London. Alison eventually joined Colt's firm, first working as a construction superintendent and later as his associate.

While working with Colt (and briefly with Alister MacKenzie), Alison was involved with most of Colt's projects, including Sunningdale, Wentworth and redesigns at two members of the current British Open rotation, Royal St. George's and Royal Lytham and St. Anne's.

Alison is most noted for his solo work while on an extended Far East swing in the early 1930s, creating such world-renowned courses as Kasumigaseki Golf Club (East), Hirono Golf Club and Kawana Golf Club. He also oversaw work on North American Colt and Alison designs such as Timber Point Golf Club, Knollwood Country Club, Milwaukee Country Club, Westwood Country Club, Sea Island Golf Club, Century Golf Club and Fresh Meadow Golf Club.

23

Thirteenth Hole, Sea Island Golf Club, Sea Island Beach, Georgia, Par-4, 375 Yards
One of the first premier resort courses in America was Sea Island, seen here in a 1932 photograph. Colt and Alison opened it for play in 1928.

"In planning a golf course there are no fixed rules to which is the compulsory to conform, and the variety which results is one of the greatest charms of the game."
— C.H. Alison

Timber Point Golf Club

Painstakingly constructed over the course of two years, Timber Point Golf Club was Harry Colt and C.H. Alison's American masterpiece. Situated on Long Island's Great South Bay, one hundred acres of the original site were marshland that Colt and Alison reclaimed and filled with beach sand. The front nine traveled through a dense forest, with enormous bunkers protecting the fairways and greens. The eighth and ninth holes emerged from the trees and played through sand and marshland before returning to the clubhouse. The entire back nine was played on the Point, with the highlights being the 140-yard par-3 twelfth and the 200-yard par-3 fifteenth (both pictured here). The fifteenth was patterned after the famous "Gibralter" hole at Moortown in Yorkshire, England. The par-4s at eleven and fourteen played to multiple fairways amongst the sand dunes. The par-4 sixteenth and 425-yard seventeenth played into the wind along the edge of the bay, with fairways surrounded by beach sand. The par-5 eighteenth required a long cape-like carry over marsh and sand. Timber Point struggled through the Great Depression and World War II and was eventually sold to Suffolk County which turned it into a 27-hole facility with little remaining today of the Colt and Alison design.

Fifteenth Hole at Timber Point Golf Club, Great South Bay, New York, Par-3, 200 Yards
The famed "Gibralter," a hole similar to the Redan in playing characteristics.

Twelfth Hole at Timber Point Golf Club, Great South Bay, New York, Par-3, 140 Yards
A short par-3 over water and marsh to an island green. The par-3 fifteenth green is in the distance to the left.

HERBERT LEEDS

(1854-1930)

A true Renaissance man, Herbert Leeds graduated from Harvard where he was an outstanding athlete in both baseball and football. As Leeds grew older he became a noted yachtsman and wrote three books, one detailing his exploits as a crew member on a competitive yachting team; the other two on the art of card-playing.

His first design effort for the Myopia Hunt Club was his masterpiece and a major influence on Golden Age architects. Similar to Donald Ross at Pinehurst, Leeds lived near the course and constantly refined Myopia in a quest for perfection. Myopia's design was one of the first to play strategically difficult for the better players while leaving more room for shorter hitters.

Leeds also designed Essex Country Club and Bass Rocks Golf Club, both in Massachusetts. The effect of Leeds on American architecture cannot be underestimated since so many architects were influenced by Myopia and its abundance of hazards. Although Leeds may have been excessive in his use of bunkers (Harry Vardon complained about them in his book *My Golfing Life*), men like Donald Ross, A.W. Tillinghast and George Thomas were influenced by Leeds' ability to place hazards.

25

26

WALTER TRAVIS

(1862-1927)

Even though he didn't take up the game until he was thirty-five, Australian Walter Travis was one of the great players in the early 20th century, winning the U.S. Amateur in 1900, 1901, and 1903. He also won the 1904 British Amateur and contended in several early U.S. Opens before turning his attention to other aspects of the game.

Though many of his Golden Age contributions were redesign efforts, it was Travis' clout as a writer and editor that may have been his greatest gift. Author of two of the earliest golf instruction books (*The Art of Putting* and *Practical Golf*), Travis founded *The American Golfer* magazine, where he served as editor for many years. Included in *The American Golfer* were articles on golf architecture, some of which were not exactly complimentary about certain styles, particularly geometric and penal courses.

Travis' finest design effort was a 1922 overhaul of Devereux Emmet's Garden City Golf Club design. Garden City contains many of the features found in the prominent inland British courses, including rugged native grasses, windblown sand pits and several pot bunkers. Travis also oversaw the original 1922 design of Westchester Country Club, host to the annual PGA Tour event. However his favorite design was a collaboration with his mentor, John Duncan Dunn, at the little-known Ekwanok Golf Club in Vermont.

HENRY FOWNES & WILLIAM FOWNES ⁽¹⁸⁵⁶⁻¹⁹³⁵⁾ ⁽¹⁸⁷⁸⁻¹⁹⁵⁰⁾

(1856-1935)
(1878-1950)

Responsible for one of America's truly great golf courses, Henry and William Fownes created and groomed Oakmont Country Club for over fifty years. Situated in the suburbs of Pittsburgh, Pennsylvania, Oakmont is a frequent host of major championships and is one of the elite clubs in the golf-rich state of Pennsylvania.

Henry Fownes formed Oakmont in 1903 after selling his steel company to Carnegie Steel. Fownes routed and designed the original course, but over the years his son William tinkered with the original design, creating the course that Oakmont is today. William Fownes was a fine player, winning the 1910 U.S. Amateur and captaining the first Walker Cup team in 1922. He also served as USGA president in 1925-26.

Oakmont's place in the history of architecture is unique. It began as a strictly penal golf course, with furrowed bunkers designed to ruin a score. But largely under the supervision of William Fownes and longtime superintendent Emil Loeffler, Oakmont took on many of the strategic and natural design characteristics of other Golden Age layouts.

W.C. Fownes

27

Eighteenth at Oakmont Country Club, Pittsburgh, Pennsylvania, Par-4, 450 Yards
The long finishing hole at Oakmont. The creation of Henry and William Fownes, Oakmont was a landmark American course and evolved from a penal design with furrowed bunkers into a strategic layout on par with other Golden Age designs.

Furrowing of bunkers at Oakmont in the early years was eventually deemed too penal. After the 1925 U.S. Open at Oakmont, even Bobby Jones wrote an essay about the unfairness of furrowed bunkers.

"The Oakmont furrows seemed to say, 'Well, here you are in a bunker, and it doesn't matter how good you are, or how much nerve you have, the only thing you can do now is blast.' Yet, a furrowed bunker, supposedly to reward a skillful player, absolutely precludes the use of a recovery shot requiring more than the application of a strong back and a willing heart! I should never care to argue for anything which would lessen the difficulty of the game, for its difficulty is its greatest charm. But when, in spite of the vast improvement in the ball, in seeking to preserve the difficulty and to make scoring as hard as it was in the old days, we make the mistake of destroying the effect of skill and judgment in an important department, I cannot help protesting."

— *Bobby Jones*

The famous "church pews" of Oakmont, another result of the strong belief by course founder W.C. Fownes that "a shot poorly played should be irrevocably lost."

CHAPTER TWO

THE NATIONAL SCHOOL OF DESIGN

"American golfers owe a debt of gratitude to Charles Blair Macdonald, who was not only the first United States Amateur Champion but the father of golf architecture in America."

— *Alister MacKenzie*

Of all the schools of design, none was more significant to the Golden Age than "The National School of Design." Oddly though, Charles Blair Macdonald and disciples Seth Raynor, Charles Banks and Devereux Emmet, are among the least recognized of the master golf architects.

The National School of Design was born out of Macdonald's desire not only to import golf to the United States, but also to design golf courses comparable to those abroad. Macdonald was arguably the father of American golf, though his Western roots in Chicago may have precluded proper recognition of his achievements. He was a pioneer rules authority, philosopher, architect and leader of the game, not to mention the first United States Amateur Champion.

Though many of the other design schools featured in this book may have taken architecture to more sophisticated levels, it was Macdonald's work that initiated the Golden Age with his combination of strategy and replicas of the great holes of Britain.

In the early 1900's, C.B. Macdonald prepared to create his ideal golf course. He returned to Scotland where he had attended St. Andrews University, determined to study and map out the very best holes. Macdonald's ideal course incorporated the strategy of the best holes from the British Isles (plus one in France). The concept of an "Ideal Golf Course" had been building for years in the back of his mind but never really came to fruition until Bernard Darwin and Horace Hutchinson printed a discussion of the best holes in the British edition of *Golf Illustrated*.

Macdonald's idea was to design a course that had no weak holes and which could be enjoyed by all skill levels of golfers. When he set out to build The National Golf Links in 1907, Macdonald built three tee-boxes on each hole and intentionally made the fairways extremely wide (75 yards in places). He created numerous playing options on each hole, with no definitive line of play. Diagonal carries from the tee were also incorporated frequently, which allowed for each golfer to establish his own line of play relative to his skill or the existing playing conditions.

The creation of strategic design by C.B. Macdonald has not been recognized for rather odd reasons. One explanation is that a famous architect from the forties and fifties labeled Macdonald's work as "penal," and that label stuck for too long of a time. C.B. Macdonald's designs were everything but penal in their intentions.

Another reason for the lack of respect for Macdonald's work may have been his use of "replicas" at The National and in his other subsequent designs. But even a brief analysis of Macdonald's replicas shows that he made major modifications and improvements to these "copies" in his own versions. Also, Macdonald never forced a replica onto a piece of property unsuited for that particular type of hole.

Following the opening of The National Golf Links in 1911, Macdonald designed Piping Rock and Sleepy Hollow for friends. He also carried out designs (all with Seth Raynor handling engineering and construction duties) at St. Louis Country Club and for the Greenbrier Resort in West Virginia.

Macdonald and Raynor later took on their most challenging project with the creation of the Lido Country Club on Long Island. Macdonald was losing interest in architecture at the time, but the challenge of building on a seaside site was too tempting. He laid out the course and left the details to Raynor, even crediting Raynor for the success of the project years later. That praise, along with fifteen solo designs under his belt, launched Seth Raynor's career. After Raynor's death, his understudy Charles Banks launched his own career, and though it was never as successful as Raynor's, it did produce several fine courses.

Charles Blair Macdonald
Pioneer of golf and course design in America and creator of The National Golf Links.

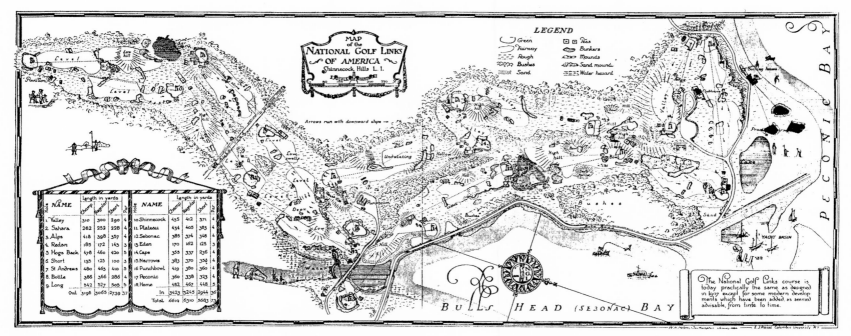

"There are many features about The National Links which will make the course famous; for example, the undulating putting greens, the absence of blind holes — nearly every tee commands a view of the entire length of the hole — and the size of the bunkers. But the main achievement is that a course has been produced where every hole is a good one and presents a new problem. That is something which has never yet been accomplished, even in Scotland, and in accomplishing it here, Mr. Macdonald has inaugurated a new era in golf."

— *H.J. Whigham*

**Fourth Hole at The National Golf Links,
Southampton, New York, Par-3, 182 Yards**
*Said the North Berwick caddie to Mr. Macdonald
when he was on the quest for ideal holes for the
National Links, "Here's the hole that makes a man
think."*

*"Take a narrow tableland, tilt it a little from right
to left, dig a deep bunker on the front side, approach
it diagonally, and you have the Redan. At North
Berwick, of course, all these things were done in the
beginning by nature. The only original thing that the
greenkeeper did was to place the tee so that the shot
had to be played cornerwise, so to speak, instead of
directly down the tableland. And when you come to
think of it that is the secret of most of the great holes
all over the world. They all have some kind of a twist."*
— *C.B. Macdonald*

34

**Sixth Hole at The National Golf Links,
Southampton, New York, Par-3, 135 Yards**
The "Short" Hole by C.B. Macdonald.

*"Putting greens to a golf course are what the face is
to a portrait. The clothes the subjects wears, the
background, whether scenery or whether draperies —
are simply accessories; the face tells the story and
determines the character and quality of the portrait
— whether it is good or bad. So it is in golf; you can
always build a putting green. Teeing grounds, hazards, the fairway, rough, etc., are accessories."*
— *C.B. Macdonald*

Fourteenth at The National Golf Links, Southampton, New York, Par 4, 355 Yards

"Wind I consider the finest asset in golf; in itself it is one of the greatest and most delightful accompaniments in the game. Without wind your course is always the same, but as the wind varies in velocity and from the various points of the compass, you not only have one course but you have many courses."

— *C.B. Macdonald*

Tenth Hole at the Greenbrier Resort Old White Course, White Sulfur Springs, West Virginia, Par-3
Macdonald and Raynor's redesign work is seen in this view of the par-3 tenth at the Greenbrier.

Fifth at Mid-Ocean Club, Tuckers Town, Bermuda, Par-4, 400 Yards
The famous "Cape" hole at Mid-Ocean tees off over Mangrove Lake and plays to a green perched above the water. The concept of the Cape, where the player who bites off as much as he can handle, has been emulated more than any other concept in golf architecture.

Aerial View of Lido Country Club, Long Beach, New York

The Lido course by Macdonald and Raynor took up 115 acres, cost $750,000 to build and required fill of over 2 million cubic yards of sand.

"Lido will stand as Seth Raynor's monumental piece of construction, a Herculean task, requiring a course to be practically raised from the sea - unless in time, his course at Yale University takes its place."
— *C.B. Macdonald*

Third Hole at Lido Country Club, Long Beach, New York, Par-3, 160 Yards

"The third hole is a copy of the Eden, or the eleventh, at St. Andrews in Scotland. The only point here is that the bank protecting the green has been made much steeper than that at St. Andrews or the other holes built in this country modeled after the eleventh at St. Andrews."
— *C.B. Macdonald*

38

Eighth Green at Lido Country Club, Long Beach, New York, Par-3, 160 Yards
"A golf hole, humanly speaking, is like life, in as much as one cannot judge justly of any person's character the first time one meets him. Sometimes it takes years to discover and appreciate hidden qualities which only time discloses, and he usually discloses them on the links. No real lover of golf with artistic understanding would undertake to measure the quality or fascination of a golf hole by a yard-stick, any more than a critic of poetry would attempt to measure the supreme sentiment expressed in a poem by the same method. One can understand the meter, but one cannot measure the soul expressed. It is absolutely inconceivable."
— *C.B. Macdonald*

Seventeenth Fairway at Lido Country Club, Long Beach, New York, Par-5, 540 Yards
Macdonald and Raynor's par-5 that included elements of the fourteenth at St. Andrews. The large cross bunker the golfers are playing over is placed in similar fashion to the Hell bunker at St. Andrews.

"The seventeenth is another composite hole, based chiefly on the principle of bunkers in echelon. The player who makes a great carry can run down through the valley and get a fine second shot, making an easy approach to the green, while one who takes a shorter way is confronted with undulations which make the shot more or less difficult. There is a carry over a deep cross bunker some 350 yards from the tee that necessitates a good drive and a good second."

— *C.B. Macdonald*

40

Fifth Hole at Yale University Golf Course, New Haven, Connecticut, Par-3, 135 Yards
The "Short" hole at Yale with 12-foot deep bunkers surrounding the entire green.

Ninth Hole at Yale University Golf Course, New Haven, Connecticut, Par-3, 225 Yards
The "Biarritz" at Yale tees off over Greist Pond to an enormous green with a large swale running through it. The concept of the Biarritz was modeled after Willie Dunn's third hole at the Golf De Biarritz in France.

"I read a golf article not long since in which the writer called a 'fetish' the copying of holes from the classical courses of Great Britain, holes which have the testimony of all great golfers for more than a century or two past as being expressive of the best and noblest phases of the game. Architecture is one of the five fine arts. If the critic's contention is true, then architecture must be a 'fetish,' as the basis of it is the copying of Greek and Roman architecture, Romanesque and Gothic, and in our own times among other forms, Georgian and Colonial architecture. One must have the gift of imagination to successfully apply the original to new situations. Surely there is nothing 'fetish' about this. I believe in reverencing anything in the life of man which has the testimony of the ages as being unexcelled, whether it be literature, paintings, poetry, tombs — even a golf hole."

— *C.B. Macdonald*

41

CHARLES BLAIR MACDONALD

Born: November, 1855 in Niagara Falls, Ontario, Canada
Died: April, 1939 in Southampton, New York
Career Summary
Born to wealthy Chicago family, father was Scottish, mother Canadian
Attended St. Andrews University, 1872-1874
Became friend of Old Tom Morris and developed as a fine player during St. Andrews stay
Laid out seven holes in 1892 for U.S. Senator Charles B. Farwell
Created first 18-hole course in U.S. in 1893 (original Chicago Golf Club site in Belmont)
Worked as a stockbroker, moved to New York in 1900 and became partner in C.D. Barney & Co.
Coined term "golf architect" in 1901
Spent several years putting together plans for "the ideal course"
Opened The National Golf Links of America in 1911
With Seth Raynor, designed several other courses
Father of American Golf Course Architecture, first rules authority and one of five creators of USGA

42

Other Interests
Stock speculating
Published Writings
Scotland's Gift—Golf (1928)
Several magazine articles on various subjects of golf and course design including several about The National Golf Links
Career Influences
The Old Course at St. Andrews, Old Tom Morris, North Berwick, Prestwick, 17th and 18th century landscape architects Humphrey Repton and Prince Puckler
Golfing Ability
First national amateur champion (1895), one of the best players in early American golf, low amateur in 1900 U.S. Open

Methodology
Drew plans, routed holes, and handled artistic side of design. Hired Raynor to handle engineering and construction details. Macdonald never charged for his design work and in several cases, did the design as a favor to close friends.
Design Characteristics
First American architect to incorporate strategic design. Set stage for "Golden Age." Built holes based on principles of great holes overseas, especially Redan, Alps and Biarritz. Used vast areas of sand and numerous bunkers. Bunkers deep and placed to dictate strategic play. Greens boldly contoured and large, favoring putting skill.
Best Original Designs (all with Seth Raynor assisting)
The National Golf Links (1911)

Piping Rock (1913)
St. Louis Country Club (1914)
The Greenbrier (Old White) (1915)
Lido Golf Club (1917)
The Links (1919)
Mid-Ocean Golf Club (1924)
The Creek Club (1925)
Yale University (1926, consultant to Raynor)
Quote
"The National has now fulfilled its mission, having caused the reconstruction of all the best known golf courses existing in the first decade of this century in the United States, and, further, has caused the study of golf architecture resulting in the building of numerous meritorious courses of great interest throughout the country."

SETH RAYNOR

Born: May 7, 1874 in Manorville, New York
Died: January 26, 1926 in West Palm Beach, Florida
Career Summary
Graduate of Princeton with a degree in engineering
Owned and operated surveying/landscaping business in Southampton
Hired by C.B. Macdonald in 1907 to handle engineering duties on National Golf Links
Did not play golf until he met Macdonald, only played sparingly after
Completely redesigned Macdonald's Chicago Golf Club in 1923
His Redan hole and one other hole at Shinnecock Hills kept during William Flynn's 1930 redesign
Originally commissioned to design Cypress Point but died in Florida during planning stages

Other Interests
Law
Career Influences
C.B Macdonald
Golfing Ability
Average player who rarely played
Methodology
As engineer to C.B. Macdonald, took Macdonald plans and handled engineering and construction details. As architect on his own, Raynor designed and routed courses, using the set group of holes that Macdonald always incorporated into his work, along with a few of his own ideas.
Design Characteristics
Built many holes based on principles of great holes overseas, especially Redan, Alps and Biarritz. Used bunkers more sparingly than Macdonald. Bunkers deep and placed to dictate strategic play. Built many courses on difficult sites. Innovator in creating improved drainage and sound routings. Greens boldly contoured and large, favoring putting skill.

Design Work with C.B. Macdonald
The National Golf Links (1911)
St. Louis Country Club (1914)
The Greenbriar (Old White) (1915)
Lido Golf Club (1917)
The Creek Club (1925)
Yale University Golf Course (1926)
Best Solo Work
Westhampton (1915)
Camargo Golf Club (1921)
Shoreacres (1921)
Chicago Golf Club (1923)
Yeaman's Hall (1925)
Fisher's Island (1926)
Quote
"I used to think that my ears would grow to be like asses' ears, for I was always stretching them to take in every word that Mr. Macdonald uttered on the subject of golf."

Tenth Hole at Chicago Golf Club, Wheaton, Illinois, Par-3, 150 Yards

A short par-3 over water by Raynor. Chicago was originally a C.B. Macdonald course, but was completely rebuilt and updated by Raynor in 1923. The tenth is a double punchbowl green seen here during play in the 1928 Walker Cup Matches.

44

Fifth Hole at Fisher's Island Golf Club, Fisher's Island, New York, Par-3, 207 Yards
Another Biarritz par-3 by Seth Raynor.

CHARLES BANKS

(1883-1931)

Charles Banks—Seth Raynor and Charles Blair Macdonald's longtime construction assistant—was involved in several of their important projects before working on his own. Banks met Raynor soon after he graduated from Yale, and later helped in the construction of his alma mater's course, a Macdonald/Raynor masterpiece.

Banks was involved in ten projects with Raynor before starting his own firm, where he designed and redesigned over thirty courses. In his solo work, Banks stuck to the trademark Macdonald/Raynor look, replete with squared-off edges to his greens, deep grass-faced bunkering and holes built on the basic principles of the great holes abroad. And just like his mentors, Banks always included a version of the "Redan" and other renowned holes in his designs. Banks' layouts of note include Forsgate Country Club (East) and Essex Country Club in New Jersey, Tamrack in New York, and his last design, Castle Harbour in Bermuda (next door to Macdonald's Mid-Ocean).

Banks also wrote several articles on design and construction and he was one of the first architects to advocate using heavy equipment for earthmoving purposes.

45

Eighteenth Hole at Castle Harbour, Tuckers Town, Bermuda, Par-3, 220 Yards

"Building a golf course and then calling in a golf architect afterwards to remedy the defects is like 'building' your own suit of clothes and then calling in a tailor to give them style and reinforce the seams so that they won't rip in vital spots. The way some golf courses rip after being built is appalling. Some courses can not safely put in a public appearance except on the darkest nights. Therefore, I believe it is safer, right at the beginning, to call in the specialist — the golf architect — and place on him the major responsibility for the designing and building of the course."

— Charles Banks

Second Hole at Castle Harbour, Tuckers Town, Bermuda, Par-4, 391 Yards
The second shot after a classic "Cape" tee shot.

Thirteenth Hole at Whippoorwill Country Club, Chappaqua, New York, Par-3, 133 Yards
A fine example of Banks' deep bunkering and boldly contoured greens.

DEVEREUX EMMET

(1861-1934)

Even though Devereux Emmet served as an advisor to his close friend C. B. Macdonald at various times during the construction of The National Golf Links, he had actually designed a fine course on his own well before Macdonald's masterpiece was constructed. Emmet was a fine player and somewhat of an American aristocrat who traveled to Europe yearly during the summer months. On one such visit Macdonald asked him to help survey several of the most famous holes of the British Isles for use in the planning of The National. His course architecture, like Macdonald's, reflected the strategies of famous holes. A trademark of sorts was his frequent use of five par-3s on many of his courses.

Opened in 1901, Garden City Golf Club remains somewhat similar to Emmet's original design, with several important changes having been made by Walter Travis after he published an article analyzing its deficiencies. Travis completely reworked the greens, rerouted some holes, and added a few features - the most famous imprint of which is the infamous Travis bunker to the left of the eighteenth green, an Eden hole. Through it all, much of the credit for Garden City's charm still goes to Devereux Emmet.

The son of a prominent judge, Emmet was a huntsman as well as a golfer and for more than twenty years would spend his springs hunting in the south where he would acquire hunting dogs. During the ensuing summers he would train the dogs out on Long Island and during the winters take his trained dogs to Ireland to sell them off. While on his "sales trips," Emmet would play the fabled courses of the British Isles. It was during one such sojourn that he spent time assisting his friend C.B. Macdonald in his quest for detailed information on the great holes.

Devereux Emmet designed over one hundred courses during his career, including many layouts on private estates, Congressional in Washington, D.C., and Marion Hollins' Women's National Golf Club, a course designed solely for women.

Sixteenth Hole at the Women's National Golf Club, Glen Head, New York, Par-3, 165 Yards
The course and club was conceived by Marion Hollins exclusively for women and opened in 1923.

Second Hole at Garden City Golf Club, Garden City, New York, Par-3, 120 Yards
A short par-3 over a natural sand pit.

CHAPTER THREE

THE PHILADELPHIA SCHOOL OF DESIGN

*"I remember that when I visited that truly magnificent and truly terri-
fying course, Pine Valley, I remarked to one of my hosts that if the club had
any members who were rather old or fat or unskillful, they must find it
very hard work. He scouted the notion and declared that such members
were proud as a peacock and as happy as sand boys if they went around
in 115 in place of their normal 120. That seems to show that in Philadelphia,
at any rate, the poorer golfers are not poor in the manly virtues."*
—*Bernard Darwin*

The five men who constitute the Philadelphia School of Design were
a diverse and eccentric group, yet they were all good friends and the
success of each can be attributed in large part to their residence in the
Philadelphia area and their mutual friendship. George Crump, Hugh
Wilson, A.W. Tillinghast, George Thomas and William Flynn were
the five founders of the Philadelphia School, and each made an
indelible mark on the landscape of American golf architecture.

How and when the Philadelphia School began is not known and is
not relevant. One likely impetus was the lack of interesting golf architecture in the Philadelphia area, which was, however, home to a host
of excellent golfers. There was a vigorous country club scene and thus
plenty of fertile ground for the fast-growing sport of golf. But there
was little to be found in the way of engaging golf course design.

One early design in the area was George Thomas' Whitemarsh
Valley. The Thomas family had given up their estate in Chestnut Hill
for the creation of a country club, with the lone stipulation that the
thirty-two year-old Thomas be allowed to lay out the new course. The
following year Thomas' fellow Philadelphia Cricket Club member,
A.W. Tillinghast, was commissioned by family friends to construct
the Shawnee Country Club on the Delaware River.

It was not until 1912 that the possibilities of golf architecture
became clear to the Philadelphians when two of the most important
projects in the history of course design were undertaken. Hugh
Wilson, a fine player from Ardmore and friend of Thomas and
Tillinghast, was commissioned by his home club, Merion Cricket
Club, to find a suitable site for a new course. Wilson was also given
the job of designing the course and he spent seven months overseas

inspecting the best of Great Britain at the recommendation of C.B. Macdonald. Wilson brought back several fresh ideas and the eventual construction of the Merion Cricket Club's East Course was profoundly influential for everyone involved in Philadelphia golf.

At around the same time, George Crump sold his hotel and convinced several men, including George Thomas, to invest in a new course he wanted to build east of Philadelphia just across the New Jersey border. From late 1912, when 184 acres were purchased for $50 per acre, until his death in 1918, George Crump designed, financed and supervised construction of Pine Valley. Each member of the Philadelphia School, including a young newcomer from Massachusetts, William Flynn, would become involved with Pine Valley in some manner. It was their most visible classroom and the inspiration that made the Philadelphia School of Design, if not the most prolific, certainly the most creative, daring and influential of all the schools of design.

Pine Valley Golf Club

"Mr. Crump was anxious to see a golf course embodying his ideas of the game and he discovered the possibilities, invisible to many others at that time, of the tree-covered stretch of land, and in the face of many discouragements he went ahead. Nothing was left to chance, and the result is that to a surprising degree his ideas have found material form. I remember that when I first played the course I loved it because I thought that it embodied many of my ideals, but I soon discovered that it embodied many more of which I had never thought at all."

—*Chick Evans*

The Pine Valley story is similar to many tales of early American golf clubs: a group of devoted golfers becomes bored with their local country club course so they band together in search of a new site devoted to pure golf and set out to build a dream layout. But that is where comparisons between Pine Valley and all others end. Certainly, the property that Pine Valley Golf Club is situated on is unique, and a course built there by anyone else would have been very good. But Pine Valley is exceptional. Its unique blend of holes and singular design traits are the result of the passion and perseverance of one man: George Crump.

How Crump discovered the site has long been a matter of debate. Did he find it while taking the train to Atlantic City, or was it property where he and his father used to hunt? Or a combination of both? Regardless, Crump discovered the site and saw its possibilities at a time when building inland courses on sandy soil was still considered questionable.

Once the acquisition details were ironed out and enough investors had signed up for memberships, Crump took charge of Pine Valley, devoting the next five years of his life to building and designing the course until his unexpected death in 1918. Even after he passed away, Crump's legacy was preserved by friends Hugh Wilson, Alan Wilson, William Fownes and Simon Carr, who all worked to carry out his design intentions and to open the completed 18-hole course in 1918.

Pine Valley endures because of Crump's vision. He did not stubbornly design the course by himself. He did not struggle to convince a committee of his worthiness as a designer nor did he have to plead for patience from his fellow founding partners while he took his time refining the design to perfection. It endures because Crump sought the advice of virtually every prominent architect and golf luminary possible.

Pine Valley is a superlative design because George Crump had the opportunity to solicit advice from so many diverse men and he knew how to weed out the good ideas from the bad ones (and there surely must have been both). With the input of talented men like H.S. Colt, A.W. Tillinghast, Hugh Wilson, George Thomas, Walter Travis and many others, Crump was able to take Pine Valley from its probable status as a very fine course, to being perhaps the greatest architectural accomplishment of the Golden Age.

"The Pine Valley course to a greater degree than any course I have ever seen possesses individuality. Everywhere this individuality was shown, no where more than on the greens, but Mr. Crump worked constantly on the whole landscape garden as if it were a picture, adding the needed touch here and there with the patience of an artist. It was pleasant to see the varicolored bushes that marked the line of play, which were but one of many refinements."

— *Chick Evans*

Aerial View of Pine Valley, 1925
A revealing view of the great Pine Valley. The front nine is featured in this photograph, with the first green and the well-bunkered second fairway at the extreme lower left. The seventh hole and "Hell's Half Acre" are visible in the upper right of the photograph.

54

Second Hole at Pine Valley Golf Club, Pine Valley, New Jersey, Par-4, 352 Yards
"These superb hazards are a part of nature. Where does art begin?"
— *Robert Hunter*

Third Green at Pine Valley Golf Club, Pine Valley, New Jersey, Par-3, 184 Yards, Circa 1922

Robert Hunter writes of Pine Valley's third: "There is no hole more exacting and thrilling to play well than this one of 184 yards. From the tee the green looks like an oasis in a desert. An absurdly small oasis, although every detail of it can be seen. The green is admirably modeled and of a beautiful design."

Fifth Green at Pine Valley Golf Club, Pine Valley, New Jersey, Par-3, 226 Yards
View from the fifth tee, circa 1922. H.S. Colt was largely responsible for the placement of this green.

"Again what a memorable short hole is the fifth — one full spoon shot over a tremendous chasm stretching from tee to green, a wilderness of fir trees on the right, big bunkers on the left. To land the ball on that green — and there is no reason in the world why you should not do it if you are not frightened — provides a moment worth living for."

— *Bernard Darwin*

"Hell's Half Acre," Seventh Hole at Pine Valley Golf Club, Pine Valley, New Jersey, Par-5, 551 Yards
View of the second shot carry, also known as Hell's Half Acre, circa 1922. A.W. Tillinghast, a friend of Crump, frequent visitor to Pine Valley, and member of the first foursome to play the course with Crump, once said: "I was one of the first to walk the property with him, and that George Crump finally incorporated two of my conceptions entirely, the long seventh and the thirteenth, will ever be the source of satisfaction."

Eighth Hole at Pine Valley Golf Club, Pine Valley, New Jersey, Par-4, 303 Yards
View of the approach shot, circa 1922.

"What we Britons were disposed to criticize was the almost fantastic severity of the traps guarding some of the greens. They are so close to the green, so omnipresent that it is dreadfully easy to get out of one onto another and then back again to the end of the chapter. This almost amounts to eternal punishment and eternal punishment had better be left for the day of judgement. The hole I have particularly in mind is the eighth...I should like to see the green bigger and at least a measure of Christian charity shown at the back of it in place of yet another trap."

— Bernard Darwin

Tenth Hole at Pine Valley Golf Club, Pine Valley, New Jersey, Par-3, 134 Yards
Two views (continued on page 60) of one of the world's great short par-3s, circa 1922. George Thomas called it "a superlative creation."

60

Tenth Hole at Pine Valley Golf Club, Pine Valley, New Jersey, Par-3, 134 Yards
Note the small sand pit in front of the green, which evidently evolved on its own. Here, it is merely a small trap, not the fiercely deep bunker it is today.

Thirteenth Hole at Pine Valley Golf Club, Pine Valley, New Jersey, Par-4, 433 Yards, Circa 1922
Robert Hunter writes: "There is no welcome here. This is a Redan for a long second to a green 433 yards from the tee."

Fourteenth Hole at Pine Valley Golf Club, Pine Valley, New Jersey, Par-3, 164 Yards, Circa 1922
"If one could have a course with sand dunes, with water hazards both as streams and as lakes, with fairways through virgin forests, with long, rolling contours, high plateaus, lovely little valleys to play through and to cross as hazards, one would have the superlative and almost ideal golf country. Such is Pine Valley, laid out by the master hand of that sterling sportsman, George Crump. Every true golfer loves Pine Valley. It may be censured by some as very difficult, especially from the rough; yet its charm is the lure of diversity coupled with the thrill of surmounting its varied hardships."

— George Thomas

Aerial View of Fifteenth and Sixteenth Holes at Pine Valley

1938 aerial view from rear of the long par-5 fifteenth. Par-4 sixteenth with its forced carry tee shot is on the left. The thirteenth is in the upper right corner.

"Pine Valley is, with the possible exception of Cypress Point, by far the most spectacular course in the world. I have never seen a course where the artificial bunkers have such a beautiful and natural appearance, and the undulations on the greens are excellent. On the other hand, I do not consider any course ideal unless it is pleasurable for every conceivable class of golfer."

— Alister MacKenzie

GEORGE ARTHUR CRUMP

Born: 1871 in Philadelphia, Pennsylvania
Died: January 24, 1918 in Clementon, New Jersey
Career Summary
Son of British vice-consul to America who inherited Colonnades Hotel in Philadelphia
Early member at numerous clubs including Philadelphia Country Club
Married at age 35, wife Isabelle died tragically less than a year after they were married
Sold profitable Hotel Colonnades in 1910 to build his dream course with several Philadelphians
Headed group purchasing 184 acres at Sumner, New Jersey railroad stop for $50 per acre in 1913
Spent a reported $100,000 of his own money to build Pine Valley
Lived on site at Pine Valley from 1913 until his sudden death in 1918

64

Other Interests
Hunting and fishing and taking care of his dogs
Published Writings
Brief articles in local Philadelphia papers reporting on the progress at Pine Valley
Career Influences
Courses of the British Isles, his many prominent golfing friends, and early Pennsylvania and New Jersey golf courses
Golfing Ability
Fine player, runner-up in 1912 Philadelphia Amateur and qualified for 1915 U.S. Amateur
Methodology
Devoted the last five years of his life to building Pine Valley. Did not do individual hole drawings. Hit shots to determine best locations for greens and proper distances. Consulted virtually all of the important figures in golf architecture at the time. Relied on James Govan as construction

foreman and initial Pine Valley greenkeeper.
Design Characteristics
Had strong feelings about the sequence of holes and their separation from one another. Not afraid to incorporate forced carries. Used a variety of holes requiring plenty of different shots. Built larger greens on long holes, smaller greens on short holes. Designed bold green contours, usually with a strong pitch from back to front. Believed in severe penalties for bad shots
Best and Only Original Design
Pine Valley Golf Club
Quote
"I think I have landed on something pretty fine. It is 14 miles below Camden, at a stop called Sumner, on the Reading R.R. to Atlantic City—a sandy soil, with rolling ground, among the Pines."

"Pine Valley is the only course in America which has been loved and pictured as a thing of structural beauty. It is a noble creation, a course of heroic carries; it has the rugged grandeur, the wealth of magnificent hazards that make it a playground of the gods."
— *Robert Hunter*

Pine Valley: George Crump and His Contributors

The design of Pine Valley is primarily attributable to George Crump. However, as many of the architects of the period did, Mr. Crump consulted several architects and local golfers, many of whom went on to have successful careers themselves. Here is a list of those who visited the site and who are credited with some assistance in the design and completion of Pine Valley.

George Crump
Founder, builder, major financial contributor, designed routing and holes, and oversaw construction of fourteen holes.

H.S. Colt
Spent one week surveying site with Crump during planning stages for the initial routing. Colt also made suggestions and drawings for each hole and his suggestion for the placement of the fifth hole was his primary contribution.

C.H. Alison
Representing firm of Colt, MacKenzie and Alison, met with Advisory Committee in March 1921 to discuss revisions to course. Made many suggestions. Some were implemented and most pertained to green contour design and maintenance issues.

Walter Travis
Consultant to Crump in early days.

A.W. Tillinghast
Frequent visitor to Pine Valley and friend of Crump. Claims to be responsible for "Hell's Half Acre" on the par-5 seventh and the green complex location on the par-4 thirteenth.

William Fownes and Simon Carr
Two of three members appointed to Advisory Committee to coordinate completion of the design after Crump's death. Both were very familiar with Crump's philosophy and worked diligently to protect his original design intentions.

Hugh Wilson
Consulted and was a frequent visitor in early days of Pine Valley. Was the primary architect in charge of completing course after Crump's death.

Alan Wilson
Frequent visitor to Pine Valley and primary consultant on soil and turfgrass issues during all construction years.

William Flynn
Frequent visitor during completion of the final four holes. Hired in 1928 to design an alternate green on the par-4 ninth and construct several new tees.

George C. Thomas, Jr.
One of 150 founding members of Pine Valley. Made frequent visits during construction prior to the war and traveled back to club in 1928 to consult with Flynn.

Perry Maxwell
Supervised recontouring of several greens in 1933.

65

Aerial of Pine Valley, Showing Much of the Back Nine.
Another view of Pine Valley in 1925. The thirteenth and fourteenth greens are in the lowest portion of the photograph and are surrounded by very few trees. The seventeenth hole runs along the railroad tracks with its island green surrounded by sand. It also appears to have had a right-hand alternate fairway at one time.

Hugh Wilson and Merion

"I believe that Merion will have a real championship course, and Philadelphia has been crying out for one for many years. The construction committee, headed by Hugh I. Wilson, has been thorough in its methods and deserves the congratulation of all golfers."

— *A.W. Tillinghast*

The Wilsons
Alan (left) and Hugh (right) helped complete Pine Valley after George Crump's premature death in early 1918.

Merion Cricket Club's decision in 1910 to create a new golf course in order to replace its existing course in Haverford, Pennsylvania is similar to stories of other clubs from the period. Among other things, the lively new Haskell ball was rendering many short designs obsolete and clubs wanted an "updated" design. In addition, the club was leasing its current property and wanted to own the land that they played golf on. And finally, golfers were refining their tastes and becoming aware of the role of golf course design, seeking out more stimulating courses.

However, the Merion story began to differ after the decision was made to create a new golf course in the suburb of Ardmore. One club member, Hugh Wilson, president of a local insurance agency, was willing to spend seven months abroad studying the most important courses of the British Isles. He was also wise enough to look over C.B. Macdonald's new masterpiece on Long Island on his way and to seek Macdonald's advice during construction of the Merion course. The knowledge he gained from his research, combined with his own original ideas, led to Wilson's innovative and timeless design of Merion Golf Club's East Course.

Though Merion is commonly referred to as the course where Wilson built holes that copied the principles of the great holes of Scotland, such as the Redan or the Road Hole, Merion is really a true original. To this day, there is simply no golf course that compares to Merion, and its unique character can be attributed to a combination of factors. The site for the East Course is somewhat peculiar compared to other classic courses. The routing covers every yard of an L-shaped property, with a road dissecting it into two separate sections. Merion East sits on only 125 acres, yet at no time does any hole feel cramped or forced due to land constraints. The unique bunkering was created by Hugh Wilson with much help from construction supervisor William Flynn and longtime course superintendent Joe Valentine. They are all visible to the golfer, each has a completely original character, and each serves a useful purpose.

Legend has it that Wilson would stand on the tees during construction of the holes while Valentine would adjust bed sheets on the site of proposed bunkers until Wilson was pleased with their visibility. This painstaking and creative fieldwork, combined with Wilson's redesign of several holes on the East shortly before his death, made Merion an architectural masterpiece that must have inspired his classmates from the Philadelphia School of Design.

67

68

Aerial View of Merion Golf Club East Course, 1924
The second, fifth, fourth, and eighth fairways at Merion East are in the lower left. Also on the lower side of the street are the fourth, ninth, and holes ten through twelve. This view also shows the first hole as a dogleg left before it was soon changed by William Flynn to today's famous 355-yard dogleg right.

Ninth Hole at Merion Golf Club East, Ardmore, Pennsylvania, Par-3, 190 Yards

"What I like best about Merion is the character and variety of her short holes . . . the third and ninth are of similar yardage, around one hundred and ninety, but an elevated tee makes the ninth play a bit shorter. At the same time, this green is more tightly trapped, and any considerable deviation from the correct line will more than likely result in a penalty."

— *Bobby Jones*

Twelfth Hole at Merion Golf Club East, Ardmore, Pennsylvania, Par-4, 415 Yards
Bobby Jones on Merion's bunkers: "'White faces' — the phrase coined by Chick Evans back in 1924 during the amateur championship." No photograph better demonstrates the "white faces" than this mid-1920s view of the par-4 twelfth.

Sixteenth Hole at Merion Golf Club East, Ardmore, Pennsylvania, Par-4, 435 Yards
"No one will ever play Merion without taking away the memory of number sixteen. I think though that the quarry is a trifle too much like the Dutch housewife's kitchen. In tidying up the place, the floor has been made very clean and there is no great difficulty in getting out. It might as well be just a bit harder."
— A.W. Tillinghast

Aerial View of Merion Golf Club East, Ardmore, Pennsylvania, June 1930
This view shows the back nine holes of Merion in the foreground. The fifteenth green is in the far right corner of the photo and the seventeenth in the lower left just on this side of the rock quarry.

"I must confess to an abiding affection for Merion. Perhaps it would be unnatural if I had not such a feeling. But I know it is not entirely sentiment which makes me like the golf course and look forward to a tournament there. The place and the club are used to good golf and to championships. They know how to get ready for them, and how to manage them after they are under way . . . Merion has always played a bit on the short side, and unless conditions of wind and weather make it otherwise, it will probably play a bit short this year, despite the fact that several new tees have been built to give it length. But Chick's 'white faces' will still be there guarding closely the sides of every green and fairway, making it tough for anyone who strays from the straight and narrow."
— *Bobby Jones*

HUGH IRVINE WILSON

Born: 1879 in Philadelphia, Pennsylvania
Died: February 3, 1925 in Bryn Mawr, Pennsylvania
Career Summary
Grew up in upscale Philadelphia suburb, graduate of Princeton University in 1902
Made his living in insurance; member of Merion Cricket Club
Appointed chairman of Merion committee in charge of creating new course
Spent seven months in the British Isles taking notes and making drawings of the most interesting holes on the classic courses
Oversaw construction of Merion's East course starting in 1911
Designed West Course in 1913
Was instrumental in completing design and construction of Pine Valley in 1918
Created plans for redesign of Merion in 1924 but died before he could see the completed work

73

Other Interests
Turfgrass experimentation
Published Writings
Various articles on turfgrass issues in USGA Green Section Bulletin
Career Influences
C.B. Macdonald and H.J. Whigham, British Isles courses, early Philadelphia golf courses, George Crump, George Thomas, A.W. Tillinghast, William Flynn, Joe Valentine
Golfing Ability
Single-digit handicap, captained men's golf team at Princeton
Methodology
On-site supervision, worked closely with construction supervisors. Construction foreman Joe Valentine would place white bed sheets on the sites of proposed bunkers and Wilson would check on their visibility from the tees.
Design Characteristics
No set routing parameters—fitting holes to land took priority over design "standards." Stressed bunker visibility. Greens not boldly contoured but contain steep and deceiving pitches. Incorporated many features of great holes from British Isles.
Best Original Designs
Merion Golf Club - East (1912, redesign with W. Flynn 1924-25)
Merion Golf Club - West (1913)
Cobbs Creek Municipal Golf Course (1917)
Pine Valley (1918 completion of final four holes with input from several others)
Phoenixville Country Club (9-holes, 1918)
Quote
"The members of the committee had played golf for many years but their experience in construction and greenkeeping was only that of the average club member. Looking back on the work, I feel certain that we would never have attempted to carry it out if we had realized one-half the things we did not know."

Twelfth Hole at Cobbs Creek Golf Course, Philadelphia, Pennsylvania, Par-3, 110 Yards

Just down the street from Merion is the Cobb's Creek municipal course, designed by Hugh Wilson and opened in 1917. It was one of Wilson's only other designs besides Merion. Pictured is the par-3 twelfth green, completely surrounded by water and thought to be one of the first island greens ever built.

Hugh Wilson on Merion

"The Merion Cricket Club, of Philadelphia, played golf on leased property for nearly twenty years and as is usual in this country, the land became so valuable that the club was forced to move. This experience showed the advantage of permanency; so early in 1911, the club appointed a committee (Messrs. Lloyd, Griscom, Francis, Toulim and Wilson) to construct a new course on the 125 acres of land which had been purchased. The members of the committee had played golf for many years but their experience in construction and greenkeeping was only that of the average club member. Looking back on the work, I feel certain that we would never have attempted to carry it out, if we had realized one-half the things we did not know. Our ideals were high and fortunately we did get a good start in the correct principles of laying out the holes, through the kindness of Messrs. C.B. Macdonald and H. J. Whigham. We spent two days with Mr. Macdonald at his bungalow near The National course and in one night absorbed more ideas on golf course construction than we had learned in all the years we had played. Through sketches and explanations of the right principles of the holes that formed the famous courses abroad and had stood the test of time, we learned what was right and what we should try to accomplish with our natural conditions. The next day we spent going over the course and studying the different holes. Every good course that I saw later in England and Scotland confirmed Mr. Macdonald's teachings. May I suggest to any committee about to build a new course, or to alter their old one, that they spend as much time as possible on courses such as The National and Pine Valley, where they may see the finest type of holes and, while they cannot hope to reproduce them in entirety, they can learn the correct principles and adapt them to their own courses."

—Hugh Wilson, 1916

A.W. Tillinghast

The most eccentric and fascinating character of the Golden Age was arguably Albert W. Tillinghast, another Philadelphian who was inspired by his fellow "classmates." Unlike his friends Hugh Wilson, George Thomas, and George Crump, Tillinghast became a professional architect. Even though he did not start practicing until he was in his early thirties, he became one of America's most prolific designers. Affectionately known as "Tillie," he had been a well-established player in his youth, receiving his first golf lesson from Old Tom Morris during a stay at St. Andrews in the mid-1890s.

Tillinghast received his first design job in 1907 through a family friend, Charles Worthington. Worthington reasoned that because of Tillinghast's playing ability and background in the game, he could design a golf course. And he was right.

Shawnee-on-the-Delaware, a resort situated on the Delaware River in Pennsylvania, became a popular Poconos resort due in large part to the golf course. After years of spending his family's money and playing billiards, polo, and cricket, Tillinghast finally discovered something he was good at. He devoted much of his time to designing Shawnee, drawing several routings and spending considerable energy overseeing its construction. Soon after the opening of Shawnee, Tillinghast started his own design company and by the 1920s it was flourishing.

Another significant early project for Tillinghast included 1915's San Francisco Golf Club, with its bold, sand-faced bunkering. Two years later, he built Somerset Hills Golf Club in New Jersey with deep, grass-faced pits and quirky mounding. No two golf courses could be more different in appearance, yet it was this variety that made Tillinghast one-of-a-kind during the Golden Age. While Ross and MacKenzie would define a trademark look for many of their courses, Tillinghast adapted his style to the setting or perhaps his particular mood at the time.

After Tillinghast's 36-holes at Baltusrol Golf Club opened in 1922, New York Athletic Club officials commissioned Tillinghast to "give them a man-sized course" on their attractive Westchester County property. He actually gave them two man-sized courses at Winged Foot—the East and West—which differ completely from the look and style of Baltusrol, yet each has proved timeless.

By the late 1920s, Tillinghast was a millionaire due in large part to his marketing talent and the unusual method he used for design remuneration. He commonly charged clients as much as ten percent of the construction fees, a remarkable sum those days. By 1930, his resume of classic courses included many other well-known gems: Ridgewood in New Jersey, Sleepy Hollow and Quaker Ridge in New York, and Brook Hollow in Texas; and redesigns of Newport in Rhode Island and Brooklawn in New York.

While he was designing courses, Tillinghast wrote prolifically on many subjects, ranging from the basics of golf architecture to tournament updates and other important golf topics of the day. Tillinghast

A.W. Tillinghast Consults with his Foreman on Site.
He once wrote, "Don't be afraid to ask your architect questions, for if he is a true master of his craft he will not only welcome them but also discuss them. Surely I have had some queer theories advanced and some truly absurd suggestions have prompted a short answer. It is a bad habit and as I grow older I am trying to break it."

had a less serious side as well. His columns on golf fashion and humorous golfing tales revealed the versatile, fun-loving side to Tillinghast. He never actually published a book on golf architecture, but he did self-publish two books of his short stories, *Cobble Valley Golf Yarns* in 1915 and *The Mutt* in 1925. Each has its moments of sentiment and humor.

In his later years Tillinghast served as a consultant to the PGA of America on golf course maintenance and design, driving to various courses and writing reports on how to save money and improve layouts. He had lost most of his money during the Depression and was losing interest in golf architecture. His final design effort, four municipal courses at Bethpage State Park in New York, were built in 1936 and are considered by many to comprise the finest municipal golf complex in the United States. Tillinghast's involvement was limited, however, and design credit should also be given to New York State Engineer Joe Burbeck.

In 1937, Tillie moved to George Thomas' hometown of Beverly Hills, California, where he and his wife Lillian opened an antique shop. Tillinghast briefly advertised a golf design partnership with California course architect William P. "Billy" Bell, but because of the sluggish golf market in California, their collaboration resulted in only a few projects.

The unfortunate ending to Tillinghast's life should not overshadow his role in the history of golf architecture. He was one of the profession's most interesting characters and he was one of golf architecture's great originals.

Aerial View of Shawnee Country Club, Tillinghast's First Design. Constructed in 1907, Shawnee is Located on the Delaware River in Pennsylvania.

"A round of golf should provide eighteen inspirations — not necessarily thrills, for spectacular holes may be sadly overdone. Every hole may be constructed to provide charm without being obtrusive with it."

— *A.W. Tillinghast*

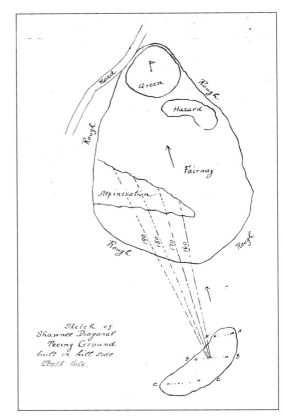

Tillinghast Sketch of Proposed Hole for Shawnee.

Compared to his later work, the strategy and general style of this drawing is quite primitive.

Aerial View of the San Francisco Golf Club, Circa 1928.

Opened in 1915, San Francisco contains some of the grandest hazards ever built. This view shows the eastern portion of the course, with the clubhouse in the upper right corner. The holes in the lower left corner nearest Junipero Serra Boulevard were subsequently altered by freeway expansion in the 1950s.

**Eleventh Hole at San Francisco Golf Club,
San Francisco, California, Par 3, 150 Yards**

*Some of Tillie's lacy edged bunkers, circa 1920.
Tillinghast once wrote, "I think that I will always
adhere to my old theory that a controlled shot to a
closely guarded green is the surest test of any man's
golf."*

**Second at Somerset Hills Golf Club, Beardsville,
New Jersey, Par-3, 180 Yards**

*The Redan hole at Somerset Hills, one of his more
daring designs.*

*"Some of the most interesting holes are those where
the best line to the flag is not direct . . . The Redan
hole at North Berwick offers a striking example of
the feature referred to. This famous hole has been
copied frequently on American courses, and some of
the efforts have resulted in very good holes, too, even
though they may differ considerably from the original. But the entrance to the Redan green is from the
right and the green slopes considerably on the
extreme left. 'Falls away' better expresses it."*
— A.W. Tillinghast

Twelfth at Somerset Hills Golf Club, Beardsville, New Jersey, Par-3, 150 Yards

A.W. Tillinghast's wonderful short par-3 at Somerset Hills sits at the lowest point on the golf course and requires a forced carry over water. Tillinghast was always a bit leery of water on his courses: "When ground for a golf course is selected, the committee is rather sure to cast their eyes around in search of water. A natural lake is regarded as a gift of the gods, and any sort of running stream meets with approval. Sometimes this great desire for water hazards has influenced committees to such an extent, when several tracts of land were available, that the property upon which the water existed was selected in preference to another, which in every other respect was more suited to the game."

MODERN GOLF ARCHITECTURE

RECONSTRUCTION AND HAZARD CREATION

WRITE FOR ILLUSTRATED BOOKLET

A·W·TILLINGHAST

25 W·45 ST· NEW YORK CITY
and
MUTUAL LIFE BUILDING
PHILADELPHIA

LILLIPUT LINKS
REG. U.S. PAT. OFF.
"minatures"

A·W·TILLINGHAST

GOLF COURSE ARCHITECT

33 WEST 42ND STREET
SUITE 836
NEW YORK

January Sixth
Nineteen Twenty Four

Mr. Fred Bacheller
The Newport Country Club.
    c/o The Casino Newport R.I.

Dear Mr. Bacheller:
    Enclosed is the checking up of the contractor's

work at the course. Will you please see that it is placed on the club

files, or with the committee. My report to the club is enclosed under

separate cover. The bill for expense of Honeyman and myself for the

dates of January 4.5.6 follows.

```
Transportation via Fall River Boat--------------------- $ 24.00
Taxi fares ----------------------------------------------   5.40
Meals --------------------------------------------------  16.25
                                                         ----------
Honeyman's fee for one day --------------------            45.65
                                                          35.00
                                                         ----------
                                                          80.65
```

Very truly yours

A.W. Tillinghast Bill for a Site Inspection at Newport Country Club

Tenth at Baltusrol Golf Club Upper Course, Springfield, New Jersey, Par-3, 180 Yards

A.W. Tillinghast writes of Baltusrol: "One of the new courses at Baltusrol furnished a splendid example of the greatly changed aspect of a shot through the removal of several prominent trees close by the green. The hole in question is the tenth on the new Upper Course. The green is situated upon the top of a knoll and the line of play is slightly across the slope. When the several trees were removed, particularly one old wild-cherry, the distance immediately appeared longer than the iron-length, which it is."

Fourth at Baltusrol Golf Club Lower Course, Springfield, New Jersey, Par-3, 104 Yards
One of the most famous par-3s in America. This is the hole in Tillinghast's version at 104 yards with a smaller, steeply-pitched and well-bunkered green.

"The merit of any hole is not judged by its length but rather by its interest and its variety as elective play is apparent. It isn't how far but how good!"
— *A.W. Tillinghast*

84

Seventeenth Hole at Baltusrol Golf Club Lower Course, Springfield, New Jersey, Par-5, 575 Yards
A view of the "Sahara" or "Hell's Half Acre" on the seventeenth.

Tenth Hole at Winged Foot Golf Club West Course, Mamaroneck, New York, Par-3, 190 Yards
Tillinghast's self-proclaimed "best par-3 I ever built" looks almost identical today.

Eighteenth Green at Winged Foot Golf Club West Course, Mamaroneck, New York, Par-4, 420 Yards
"As the various holes came to life, they were of a sturdy breed. The contouring of the greens places a premium on the placement of the drives, but never is there the necessity of facing a prodigious carry of the sink-or-swim sort. It is only the knowledge that the next shot must be played with rifle accuracy that brings the realization that the drive must be placed. The holes are like men, all rather similar from foot to neck, but with the greens showing the same varying characters as human faces."
— A.W. Tillinghast

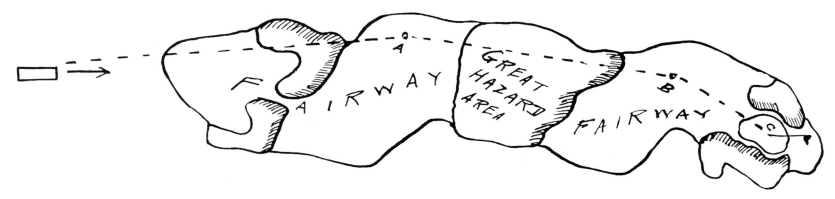

A.W. Tillinghast Sketch of a "Hell's Half Acre" Par-5
Originally inspired by the seventh at Pine Valley for which A.W. Tillinghast was partly responsible, the concept of the "Hell's Half Acre" hole is sketched and described by its creator: "In my humble opinion the green to the three-shot hole must be beyond the range of any player who misses either his drive or second stroke. Doglegging enables us to accomplish this. But the most effectual method, and I believe the only satisfactory one, is the location of a truly formidable hazard across the fairway. This must be carried with the second shot if the green is to be gained with the third. Obviously this break in the fairway must be great, let us say 100 yards, for it not only has to be crossed with the second, but also keep any shot short of it from getting home."

Advertisement for Tillinghast and Bell
When A.W. Tillinghast moved to California in the 1930s he briefly partnered with George Thomas' associate, Billy Bell.

ALBERT WARREN TILLINGHAST

Born: May 7, 1874 in Philadelphia, Pennsylvania
Died: May, 1942 in Toledo, Ohio
Career Summary
Born into a wealthy family; he once said: "I never finished a school I went to."
Nicknamed "The Terror" because of tempestuous childhood
Introduced to golf in 1890's in Scotland; took lessons from Old Tom Morris
Hired by family friends to design Shawnee Country Club in 1907; soon started design business
Worked as editor of *Golf Illustrated* for several years while becoming well-known architect
One of the founders of the PGA of America, he later consulted for the PGA
Moved to California in 1937 to open antique shop and briefly partnered with course architect Billy Bell

Other Interests
Photography: 1898 portrait of Old Tom Morris became famous (see Chapter 1). Music: loved to play the piano. Art: painting, drawing and collecting. Also collected antique furniture. Sports and games: polo, bridge, cricket and billiards

Published Writings
Cobble Valley Golf Yarns (1915)
The Mutt (1925)
Hundreds of magazine articles on various aspects of golf as well as short stories

Career Influences
The Old Course at St. Andrews and other Scottish courses, Old Tom Morris, Pine Valley/George Crump, Hugh Wilson/Merion, Donald Ross, George C. Thomas, Jr.

Golfing Ability
Scratch player who qualified for the U.S. Amateur three times and finished 25th in the 1910 U.S. Open at Philadelphia Cricket Club

Design Characteristics
Master of variety; no two Tillinghast courses look the same. Strategy was guiding principle behind most holes he built. Bunkering ranged from sand-faced to grass-faced/flat-bottomed. Emphasized naturalness in construction most of the time. Greens usually medium in size, styles range from steeply pitched to whimsical contouring. Later in life, advocated minimal bunkering and removal of all cross-bunkers.

Methodology
On early designs, spent a great deal of time on site and had well-organized construction team. In later years he made less frequent visits and simply wrote letters or drew plans.

Best Original Designs
Baltusrol Golf Club (1922, 36 holes)
Baltimore Country Club (1926, East course and routing for West)
Bethpage State Park (1935, consultant on three courses)
Brook Hollow Golf Club (1921)
Newport Golf Club (1924, redesign)
Philadelphia Cricket Club (1922, Flourtown Course)

Quaker Ridge Golf Club (1926)
Ridgewood Country Club (1929, 27 holes)
San Francisco Golf Club (1915)
Somerset Hills Golf Club (1917)
Winged Foot Golf Club (1923, 36 holes)

Quote
"When it is more generally realized that a truly fine round of golf represents the accurate fitting together of shots that bear a distinct relation to each other, with the greens opening up to best advantage after placed drives, then the game will be a truer test of all the mighty ones than so many courses now present."

87

Fourteenth Hole at Baltimore Country Club Five Farms East Course, Baltimore, Maryland, Par-5, 600 Yards

One of two very fine par-5s at Baltimore Five Farms East is described by its architect A.W. Tillinghast: "The extreme distance of this three-shotter is justified because the terrain favors long hitting. Two full shots with the wood, the second across Hell's Half Acre, brings the elevated green within reach of the short approach, which may score a bird."

Seventh Hole at Baltimore Country Club Five Farms East Course, Baltimore, Maryland, Par-4, 349 Yards

A.W. Tillinghast describes his seventh at Baltimore Five Farms East: "An exacting hole but a splendid test of the drive and controlled pitch combination. A hooked tee shot is punished severely. The green presents two levels and is very closely trapped on all sides, save for a small neck at the right front. The drive should be placed down the center."

**Aerial View of Philadelphia Cricket Club
Flourtown Course, 1939**
*The sixth green is in the lowest corner of the photo-
graph. Note the two par-5s in the center of the picture.
The fourth hole on the right included a variation of
the "Hell's Half Acre." On the left, the par-5 seventh
included some rather interesting bunkers.*

89

George C. Thomas, Jr.

Even though George Thomas was the first of the Philadelphians to design a golf course, his career did not blossom until after World War I when he moved to California. His primary motive in moving to Beverly Hills was to search for the ideal rose-growing climate to further his many experiments and hybridizing, but his passion for golf traveled with him.

Immediately after arriving in 1920, Captain Thomas joined Los Angeles Country Club. The club had hired British golf architect Herbert Fowler and was in the process of expanding to 36 holes. Because of his experience with three designs in the East, Thomas was asked by Fowler to carry out his plans. Being a relative newcomer, Thomas apparently did not have much say in the original design because six years later, in 1927, he would completely redesign the club's famed North Course.

After the first go-around at the Los Angeles Country Club courses, Thomas designed several layouts on his own, free of charge, including 36 holes for the city of Los Angeles. Because of city funding problems, Thomas used part of his personal fortune to help pay for the completion of the courses.

Soon thereafter, Thomas was joined by William P. "Billy" Bell, an engineer and construction specialist who had been working for Willie Watson. From 1925 to 1930, Thomas and Bell collaborated on eight designs, all of which were heralded at the time and some of which remain as classic tests of golf: La Cumbre Country Club, Ojai Valley Inn, Bel-Air Country Club, Baldwin Hills Golf Club, Fox Hills Golf Course, Riviera Country Club, a redesigned Los Angeles Country Club North, and Stanford Golf Club.

Twelfth at Whitemarsh Valley Country Club, Chestnut Hill, Pennsylvania, Par-3, 175 Yards
George Thomas' first design was at Whitemarsh Valley. The land once belonged to the Thomas family who sold it to the new club at a fair price under the condition that the young Thomas would design the course. The twelfth is a particularly dramatic par-3, with twenty-five foot drop off on the left.

"Wise is the man who knows how to play each hole as he should play, and skillful the golfer who can place his shots after he knows where they should go. Such a player is exceedingly hard to defeat on a course with proper strategy."

— George Thomas

92

First at La Cumbre Country Club, Santa Barbara, California, Par-4, 415 Yards
Constructed in 1925 by Thomas and Bell, La Cumbre included dramatic bunkering and several holes playing around Potter Lake.

"In golf construction art and utility meet; both are absolutely vital; one is utterly ruined without the other."
— *George Thomas*

Sixteenth Green at La Cumbre Country Club, Santa Barbara, California, Par-4, 405 Yards
A small green sitting atop a deep canyon.

94

Twelfth at Bel-Air Country Club, Los Angeles, California, Par-4, 350 Yards
Thomas and Bell's "Mae West" hole, named after the buxom film star. The more the drive was cut around the hill on the right, the better the angle to the pin.

Aerial View of Bel-Air Country Club
The eleventh green sits in the upper left-hand corner, the fifteenth green in the lower left-hand corner, and the dramatically bunkered sixteenth in the middle right of the photo. Sunset Boulevard is in the lowest right corner.

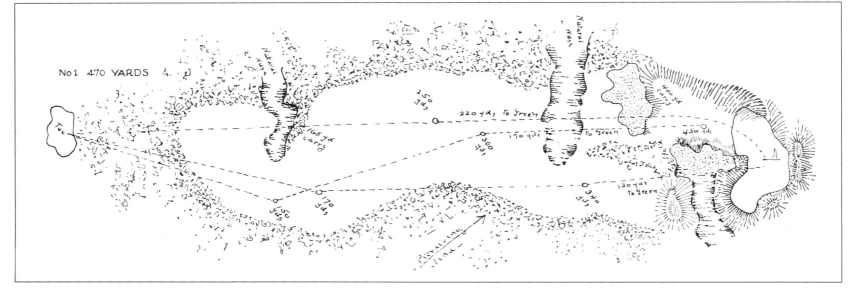

George Thomas' Sketch of the First at Riviera Showing the Various Strategic Playing Options.
"The strategy of golf is the thing which gives the short accurate player a chance with a longer hitter who cannot control his direction or distance."

— *George Thomas*

97

Second Green at Riviera Country Club, Pacific Palisades, California, Par-4, 460 Yards
"If possible, it is well to have the second hole come back to the club, so that tie matches may for the first three holes never be over the distance of one fairway from home. Also, if one is late in arriving, one may pick up friends at the third tee."

— *George Thomas*

View of Second Green and Tenth Hole at Riviera Country Club, Pacific Palisades, California
Note the famous tenth in the background before George Thomas added greenside bunkering in preparation for the 1929 Los Angeles Open.

"Length means nothing without character, but a true test must have sufficient length and character."
— *George Thomas*

Sixth Green at Riviera Country Club, Pacific Palisades, California, Par-3, 145 Yards
Thomas' infamous par-3 at Riviera with a bunker in the middle of the green. Thomas once wrote, "One shotters are most important. In these holes one gets a keener interest on the tee shot than on others because it may be placed on the green by most men."

Ninth Hole at Riviera Country Club, Pacific Palisades, California, Par-4, 420 Yards
The fairway bunkers here create numerous playing options from the tee, situated out of view to the lower right of picture.

"The strategy of the golf course is the soul of the game. The spirit of golf is to dare a hazard, and by negotiating it reap a reward, while he who fears or declines the issue of the carry, has a longer or harder shot for his second . . . yet the player who avoids the unwise effort gains advantage over one who tries for more than in him lies, or who fails under the test."

— *George Thomas*

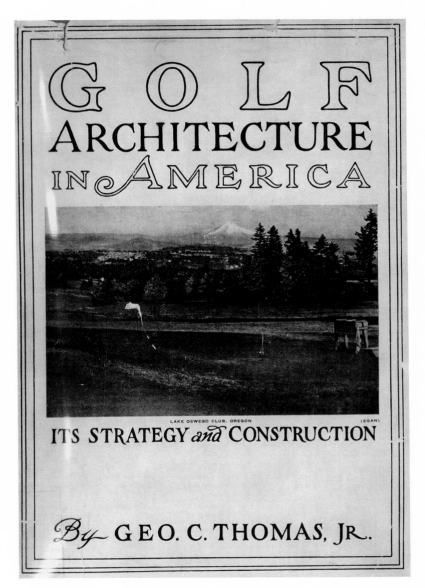

Dust Jacket for *Golf Architecture in America*
George Thomas's classic book was published in 1927, the same year his design at Riviera opened for play.

"If the average golfer considers the points of strategy which have been worked out in advance for a properly designed hole, he will undoubtedly improve his game in his play of such a problem. There is no question but that the strategy of golf is one of its most important assets, and our newer courses present many most interesting situations which increase their value. The question of strategy is of the utmost importance to the golf architect and to the golfer, and such strategy will be developed more and more during the coming years."

— *George Thomas*
from Golf Architecture in America

101

GEORGE CLIFFORD THOMAS, JR.

Born: October 3, 1873, Philadelphia, Pennsylvania
Died: February 23, 1932, Beverly Hills, California

Career Summary
Designed courses for wealthy friends in East before moving West; never charged a fee
Met and worked with other architects from the Philadelphia area, particularly Crump and Wilson
Moved to California in 1920 and worked with Billy Bell on several historic designs
Was a founding member of Pine Valley and helped William Flynn during club's 1928 alterations
Worked with Tillinghast on Philadelphia Cricket Club's Flourtown design where both men held memberships

Interests
Aviation: World War I captain, surviving three plane crashes, funded his own unit's activities. Gardening: Prolific rose hybridizer of over 40 varieties including "Dr. Huey," one of the most important rootstocks ever developed, still widely used today. Deep sea fishing: President of Tuna Club on Catalina Island, fished with author Zane Grey and once battled six hours for a swordfish and won. Dogs: Bred English Setters, won 1903 Westminster Kennel Club "Best of Breed." Other Interests: banking, swimming, hunting, tennis, flying.

Published Writings
The Practical Book of Outdoor Rose Growing (1920)
Roses For All American Climates (1924)
Golf Architecture in America (1927)
Game Fish of the Pacific, Southern Californian and Mexican (1931)
Many essays in regional magazines on golf archi-

tecture, golf rules, roses and deep sea fishing.

Career Influences
George Crump/Pine Valley, Hugh Wilson/Merion, Donald Ross, A.W. Tillinghast, H.S. Colt, Alister MacKenzie's *Golf Architecture*

Golfing Ability
Single digit handicapper who once shot 68. Shot 74 in one of his last rounds at Los Angeles Country Club South before his death.

Methodology
Thomas walked sites and even flew over them in his plane to determine routing. He made drawings, handled communications and supervised work in progress. He hit shots to prospective fairways and green sites. Billy Bell oversaw construction and handled engineering, though Thomas signed off on all green sites before seeding.

Design Characteristics
Master of strategic design and course routing. Built some of the most innovative, eccentric and

strategic holes ever seen. With Bell on his California designs, built large, sand-faced bunkers with lacy edges. Made creative use of barrancas and swales for drainage purposes. *Golf Architecture in America* is a definitive book on the subject.

Best Original Designs
Whitemarsh Valley (1907)
Ojai Valley Inn (1925)
La Cumbre Country Club (1925 redesign)
Bel-Air Country Club (1926)
Riviera Country Club (1927)
Los Angeles Country Club—North (1927 redesign)
Stanford Golf Club (1930)

Quote
"The strategy is the soul of the game."

Billy Bell

Considered soft-spoken and modest by those who knew him, Billy Bell never received the credit he deserved for his remarkable bunker shaping, his ingenuity and innovations in constructing golf courses, or his influence on George Thomas' design work.

Born on April 19, 1886, in Canonsburg, Pennsylvania, Bell emigrated to California in 1910, but did not know Thomas or the other Philadelphia School members during his years in Pennsylvania. With a background in agriculture, Bell worked first as a caddiemaster at Annandale Golf Club and later as the greenkeeper at Pasadena Golf Club. In the years before 1920, Bell worked briefly as a construction foreman for Southern California's most prominent golf course architect at the time, Willie Watson.

In 1920 Bell ventured into the design business on his own and quickly began to get work because of California's booming golf course development. Among his first designs were the Balboa Park Golf Course and San Diego Country Club. Though the exact time is unclear, Bell met George Thomas sometime around 1922, and asked for Thomas' endorsement of his work in Northern California at Candlewood Country Club.

Bell served as construction foreman on several Thomas designs. In early photographs of the courses, one can see the dramatic, rugged-edged, "baseball glove" sand traps which became known as "Thomas bunkers." Significantly, photographs of Thomas' early solo work do not show this kind of bunkering, but photographs of Bell's work in the late 1920's and 1930's reveal the same spirited bunker design. Thomas and Bell worked together on such classic courses as Bel-Air Country Club, Ojai Valley Inn, Los Angeles Country Club, Stanford Golf Club, and their masterpiece, Riviera Country Club. Bell went on to design many fine courses in the western United States, always with his trademark bunker sculpturing. Sadly, much of the original character of these bunkers has been lost through years of weather, explosion shots, and the use of motorized edgers.

Bell had a major impact on Thomas' work, and he designed or redesigned more than one hundred courses on his own. He was a charter member of the American Society of Golf Course Architects and served as its president in 1952. Bell briefly formed a partnership with A.W. Tillinghast after the noted architect moved to California in 1937. They worked on at least two projects together, a redesign of the Brookside municipal courses (which surround the Rose Bowl) and Virginia Country Club in Long Beach.

WILLIAM P. BELL AT CASTLEWOOD

Courses Under Construction	Courses Being Designed
El Caballero Country Club	
La Cumbre Country Club	Castlewood Country Club
San Pedro Golf Club	Rolling Hills Golf Club
Long Beach Municipal	Chevy Chase Golf Club
Girard Country Club	Santa Susana Country Club
Bel-Air Golf Club	

WILLIAM P. BELL

Golf Architect

MANAGER GOLF DEPARTMENT

PACIFIC PROPERTIES CORPORATION

Pacific Properties Building · · Pasadena, California

Thruout our various departments we are Equipped to Design and Construct Golf Courses, Buildings and Water Systems.

Eleventh Green at Los Angeles Country Club North Course, Los Angeles, California, Par-3, 220 Yards
Reverse Redan green at Los Angeles North. Some of Thomas and Bell's finest bunkering was created here during their 1927-28 redesign.

"Who shall say which par affords the most superlative play? No one will deny the lure, intrigue and importance of the one-shotter."
— *George Thomas*

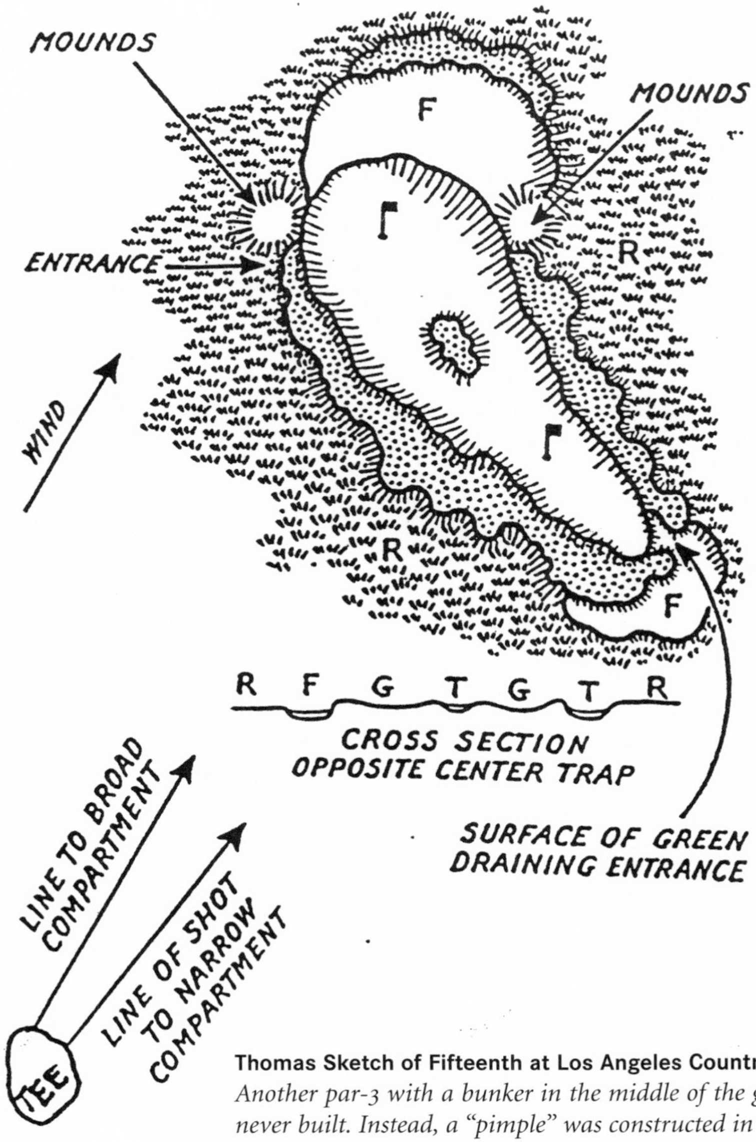

MOUNDS

MOUNDS

F

R

ENTRANCE

R

WIND

F

R

F

R F G T G T R

CROSS SECTION
OPPOSITE CENTER TRAP

SURFACE OF GREEN
DRAINING ENTRANCE

LINE TO BROAD COMPARTMENT

LINE OF SHOT TO NARROW COMPARTMENT

TEE

Thomas Sketch of Fifteenth at Los Angeles Country Club North Course
*Another par-3 with a bunker in the middle of the green, though this version was
never built. Instead, a "pimple" was constructed in place of the bunker.*

Alister MacKenzie Visits Riviera During Construction
Billy Bell (left), George Thomas (center), and Alister MacKenzie (right) pose for Scotty Chisholm's camera during a site visit by the "Good Doctor."

"I especially admire the work of Mr. George C. Thomas Jr. It is remarkably fine."
— *Dr. Alister MacKenzie*

William Flynn

The lone member of the Philadelphia school not born in Pennsylvania, William Flynn was a Massachusetts native who migrated to work on the construction of Merion Cricket Club's new course. Flynn received his first design commission at the age of nineteen and was hired in 1912 by Hugh Wilson to supervise construction of the Merion course.

William Flynn's career blossomed thanks in large part to his work at Merion and his friendship with Wilson. Though Wilson's health prevented what would have been a logical design partnership, Flynn persisted, first joining forces with a local agronomist before creating the firm of Toomey and Flynn after World War II. Howard Toomey's experience in railroad engineering somehow translated well to golf courses, as he and Flynn produced a number of fine layouts during their fourteen-year partnership.

The relationship between Toomey and Flynn presumably worked similarly to that of George Thomas and Billy Bell. Flynn, like Thomas, handled the public relations, design, and agronomic issues, while Toomey supervised the drawing of plans and the various engineering details. The result was a sound combination of art and science, particularly in the late 1920s and early 1930s when the partnership produced several daring designs featuring vast areas of sand and sometimes more than 150 bunkers to a course. Though much of their best-known work was constructed during the early and mid 1920s, a complete 1931 redesign of Shinnecock Hills Golf Club will always be their most enduring legacy to golf architecture.

Despite his New England heritage, Flynn was accepted by his peers Crump, Wilson, Tillinghast, and Thomas of the Philadelphia School. This was made clear when he was awarded a 1928 commission to add an alternate green to the ninth hole at Pine Valley. And in the ultimate show of respect to his fellow Philadelphians, Flynn asked that Pine Valley member (and then California resident) George Thomas travel east to share his expertise for the project.

Twelfth Hole at Indian Creek Club, Miami, Florida, Par-3, 200 Yards

A trademark Flynn and Toomey par-3, with bunkers left and one in the front right.

Fifth Hole at Shinnecock Hills Golf Club, Southampton, New York, Par-4, 450 Yards
Many of the vast areas of sand employed at Shinnecock were typical of Flynn's designs in treeless settings.

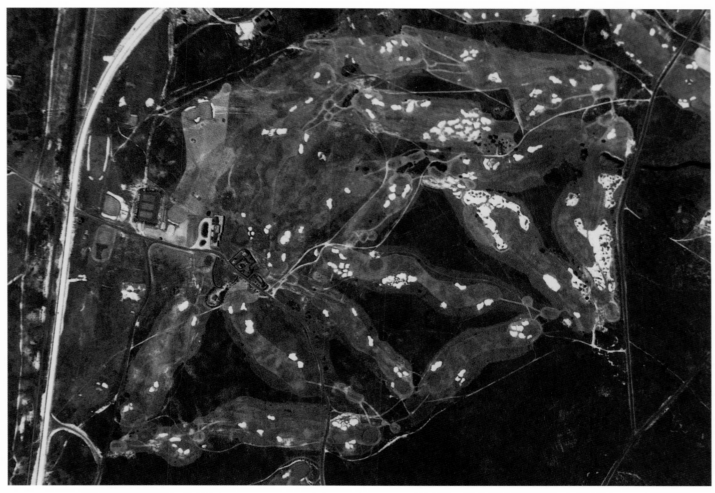

Survey Aerial View of Shinnecock Hills, Circa 1938

Architect C.H. Alison was asked by club members to evaluate William Flynn and Howard Toomey's redesign at Shinnecock. Despite the competitive nature of the design business at this point, Alison could find no fault: "The framework actually proposed does not require much general comment. The total length is adequate; the distribution of length is excellent; changes of direction are frequent; natural features are admirably used, and those not used are reduced to a bed-rock minimum...We are extremely satisfied that Mr. Flynn's plans are as good as can be made on this site and that the proposed course will prove to be of the first order."

WILLIAM STEPHEN FLYNN

Born: December 25, 1891 in Milton, Massachusetts
Died: 1945 in Philadelphia, Pennsylvania
Career Summary
Played high school golf against Francis Ouimet
All around athlete and sportsman
At 19, hired to design first course in 1909 at Hartwellville C.C. in Vermont
Worked as construction supervisor for Merion Cricket Club's East Course
Stayed on as course superintendent for short time after Merion opened in 1912
Practiced architecture briefly before war, then teamed with engineer Howard Toomey after WWI
Toomey and Flynn partnership was very productive and lasted until 1933

Other Interests
Tennis: at age of 18, taught as a professional at Lake Placid Club. Football: part-owner of Philadelphia Eagles at one time. Turfgrass research: worked as greenkeeper for many years and conducted numerous experiments.
Published Writings
Several articles for the USGA Green Section Bulletin on architecture and agronomic issues
Career Influences
Hugh Wilson/Merion, Pine Valley, early Massachusetts courses
Golfing Ability
Single digit handicapper
Methodology
Flynn and Toomey first drew layouts using topographical maps, then modified them in the field and added hazards on site or after course was open for some time. Flynn was responsible for artistic and communication side; Toomey handled engineering details.
Design Characteristics
Master of course routing. Bunkering lacked artistic flair of other Philadelphians, but was sound in strategic placement. One of the first architects to use heavy earthmoving equipment with natural-looking results. Pioneer in use of multiple tees.
Best Design Work
Lancaster Country Club (1920)
Cherry Hills Country Club (1923)
The Homestead—Cascades (1923)
Merion Golf Club—East (1925 redo with Hugh Wilson)
Rolling Green Country Club (1926)
Huntingdon Valley Country Club (1927)
Philadelphia Country Club (1927)
The Country Club (MA) (1927—remodel and addition of Primrose nine)
Indian Creek Country Club (1930)
Shinnecock Hills Country Club (1931)
The Country Club (OH) (1931)
Quote
"An architect should never lose sight of his responsibility as an educational factor in the game. Nothing will tend more surely to develop the right spirit of the game than an insistence upon the high ideals that should inspire sound golf architecture. Every course needs not be a Pine Valley or a National, but every course should be so constructed as to afford incentive and to provide a reward for high-class play; and by high-class play is meant, simply the best of which each individual is himself capable."

Fourteenth Hole at Cherry Hills Golf Club, Denver, Colorado, Par-4, 470 Yards

One of the finest par-4's in golf, even in its younger days.

"The principal consideration of the architect is to design his course in such a way as to hold the interest of the player from the first tee to the last green and to present the problems of the various holes in such a way that they register in the player's mind as he stands on the tee or on the fairway for the shot to the green."

— William Flynn, 1927

Eighteenth Hole at Cherry Hills Golf Club, Denver, Colorado, Par-4/5, 465 Yards

Flynn's version of a "Cape" hole is one of the finest finishing holes in golf. However, Flynn was not a proponent of water hazards: "One natural hazard which is more or less of a nuisance is water. This is not nearly as bad when it parallels play and forms a picturesque landscape feature of the course... Water hazards absolutely prohibit the recovery shot, perhaps the best shot in the game. On the other hand, how valuable these streams are when the greens and fairways need water."

111

Fourth Hole at Cascades Golf Club, Hot Springs, Virginia, Par-3, 195 Yards
A fine one-shotter that has characteristics of a Redan.

"The best way to whet the appetite and improve the game of any golfer is to offer an incentive and provide a reward for high class play, and by high class play is meant simply the best of which each individual is capable. Placing a premium on accuracy with due consideration for length should be the aim of all men who design golf courses, for accuracy in the play signifies skill and skill is generally the master of brute force."
— *William Flynn*

Fourth Hole at The Country Club, Brookline, Massachusetts, Par-4, 340 Yards
Toomey and Flynn added nine holes at The Country Club in 1927 and remodeled the bunkers on the existing 18 holes. The irregularly shaped bunkers seen here are some of Flynn's very best.

"The premium on accuracy should carry the greatest reward for this is the essence of any game. Carry, while slightly less valuable than accuracy is important in that it promotes boldness. Length may be considered least important but this becomes quite a factor when a player is able to mould all three tests together."
— William Flynn, 1927

Ninth Hole at The Country Club, Brookline, Massachusetts, Par-5, 505 Yards

"A concealed bunker has no place on a golf course because when it is concealed it does not register on the player's mind as he is about to play the shot and thus loses its value. The best-looking bunkers are those that are gouged out of faces or slopes, particularly when the slope faces the player. They are very much more effective in that they stand out like sentinels beckoning the player to come on or keep to the right or left."

— William Flynn, 1927

Seventeenth Hole at The Country Club, Brookline, Massachusetts, Par-4, 365 Yards
A simple two-shotter that has cost everyone from Harry Vardon to Tony Lema to Arnold Palmer chances at capturing the U.S. Open.

"All architects will be a lot more comfortable when the powers that be in golf finally solve the ball problem. A great deal of experimentation is now going on and it is to be hoped that before long a solution will be found to control the distance of the elusive pill. If, as in the past, the distance to be gotten with the ball continues to increase, it will be necessary to go to 7,500 and even 8,000 yard courses and more yards mean more acres to buy, more course to construct, more fairway to maintain and more money for the golfer to fork out."

— William Flynn, 1927

CHAPTER FOUR

THE ROSS SCHOOL OF DESIGN

Donald Ross went to St. Andrews in the early 1890s and learned from Old Tom Morris about all facets of the game. But it became apparent that architecture and greenkeeping were the two areas of most interest to young Donald. In 1893, Ross returned to serve as the club greenkeeper at his home course in northern Scotland, Dornoch. There, his tutoring continued under the watchful eye of John Sutherland, the Dornoch club secretary, who also had an interest in golf architecture.

Donald Ross emigrated to America at the turn of the century and took the job as both pro and greenkeeper at Oakley Country Club, in Watertown, Massachusetts. Ross soon converted the rather benign and dull layout into a sporty test of golf. His work so impressed James Tufts that Ross was invited to become the pro and course designer for the Tufts' family resort being built in Pinehurst, North Carolina. Word spread quickly about Ross' 1901 work at Pinehurst and he soon became known as an architect worthy of hire. Over the next forty-plus years Ross designed or remodeled nearly four hundred courses, and continued to refine his beloved Pinehurst #2 until his death in 1948.

He was a soft-spoken and humble man whose design style reflected his personality. Ross' background in Scotland, particularly at Dornoch, can still be felt in his work. He rarely strayed from his roots by building simple but strategically designed holes with bold green complexes reminiscent of Dornoch. Ross was the first architect to travel extensively, and he was the first to design courses based on only one or two site visits. And in a several cases, he made no site visits at all. However, Ross gave elaborate sketches and instructions to his construction supervisors and the results showed a remarkable attention to detail.

Variety, strategy, and naturalness were the most consistent traits in a Ross design, and he instilled these traits in the many architects he tutored. Contrary to popular belief, each of his courses contained some individuality, while still retaining obvious Ross touches. He constructed everything from punch bowl greens to crowned greens, and sand-faced bunkers to deeper, grass-faced ovals like those at Dornoch.

Donald Ross has long been considered one of the founding fathers of American golf architecture along with men such as Alister MacKenzie, A.W. Tillinghast, and C.B. Macdonald. Certainly, with so many classic designs to his credit and his role in establishing the American Society of Golf Course Architects, he is worthy of having his own school, The Ross School of Design.

Donald Ross

John Sutherland

Even though Old Tom Morris and the Old Course had a profound impact on Donald Ross the golf architect, John Sutherland of Dornoch is probably most responsible for Ross' career as a designer. He encouraged Ross to serve an internship under Old Tom, and it was Sutherland, serving as the club secretary, who brought Ross back to Dornoch as their pro and greenkeeper in the mid-1890s. Sutherland was a student of design and agronomy, and he worked closely with Ross at Dornoch until Ross departed for the United States.

118

Ninth Hole at Pinehurst Resort #2 Course, Pinehurst, North Carolina, Par-3, 162 Yards
Donald Ross tees off on the ninth after the greens have been converted to grass putting surfaces.

"Bearing in mind that golf should be a pleasure and not a penance, it has always been my thought to present a test of the player's game; the severity of the test to be in direct ratio with his ability as a player. I carried out this thought in the changes made on Number Two."

— Donald Ross

Seventeenth Hole at Pinehurst Resort #2 Course, Pinehurst, North Carolina, Par-3, 187 Yards
"The resort, which has long been recognized for its leading influence in golfing circles, took another great step forward in golf in the summer of 1935. The changes which have brought about this great transformation in Pinehurst golf are the entire elimination of sand greens and the substitution of grass putting surfaces on the Number Two Course, and the complete remodeling of the layout of this course. As a result of extensive changes, I am firmly of the opinion that the leading professionals and golfers of every caliber, for many years to come, will find in the Number Two Course the fairest yet most exacting test of their game, and yet a test from which they will always derive the maximum amount of pleasure."

— *Donald Ross*

Tenth Hole at Pine Needles Resort, Pinehurst, North Carolina, Par-4, 400 Yards
Note the sand tee box.

"...give me some slightly rolling terrain and sandy soil, and I'll give you the best courses."
— *Donald Ross*

Ninth Green at Longmeadow Country Club, Lowell, Massachusetts
"A course that continually offers problems - one with fight in it, if you please — is the one that keeps the player keen for the game."
— Donald Ross

122

Aerial View of Aronimink Golf Club in Pennsylvania, Circa 1939
The beautifully bunkered Aronimink, seen from 6,000 feet.

"I intended to make this course my masterpiece, but not until today did I realize I built better than I knew."
— Donald Ross on Aronimink

124

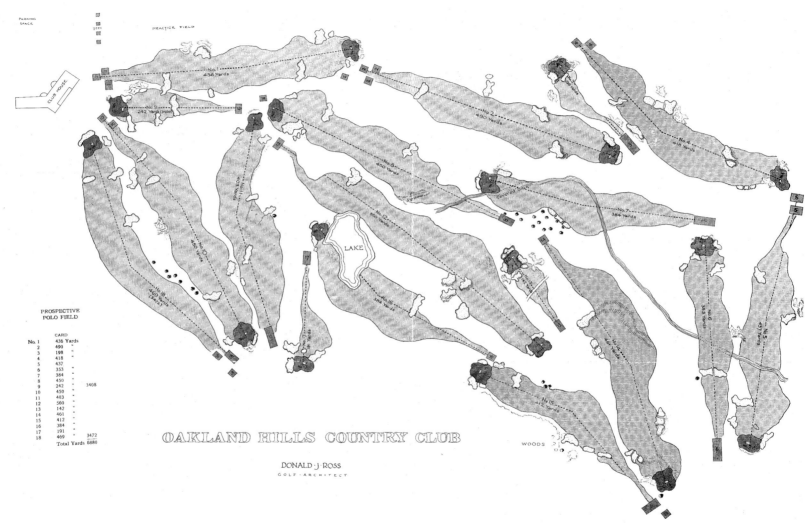

Map of Donald Ross' Oakland Hills Design Prior to Robert Trent Jones' Redesign.
"I rarely find a piece of property so well suited for a golf course."
— *Donald Ross*

Seventh Hole at Oakland Hills, Bloomfield Hills, Michigan, Par-4, 384 Yards
An interesting par-4 requiring navigation around a creek.

"Water hazards always lend welcome variety and test of skill to a course. They are pleasant breaks that can generally be made into charming beauty spots. But don't allow your enthusiasm for them to run away with your good judgment. Limit the number of water hazards to three. Two might be better. The repeated loss of balls by those here for whom the hazard is difficult is apt to create dissatisfaction."

— Donald Ross

Sixteenth Hole at Oakland Hills, Bloomfield Hills, Michigan, Par-4, 400 Yards
Resident Pro M.J. Brady is seen here demonstrating the approach shot to the famous sixteenth green at Oakland Hills. The original design included a bunker on the right side of the fairway which players negotiated if they wanted to reduce the length of the second shot.

"In building my courses, my aim is to lay out an alternate route on practically every hole. That is, in the case of a two-shot hole, the scratch player or long hitter has one way of getting home in two shots — he must place his drive accurately to do so — and the high handicapper or short hitter has another route to reach the green in three."
— *Donald Ross*

Seventeenth Hole at Oakland Hills, Bloomfield Hills, Michigan, Par-3, 191 Yards
"Variety is the spice of golf, just as it is of life."

— *Donald Ross*

Thirteenth Hole at Salem Country Club, Salem, Massachusetts, Par-4, 320 Yards
Some of Ross' most dramatic bunkering is at Salem.

"There is no such thing as a misplaced bunker. Regardless of where a bunker may be, it is the business of the player to avoid it."
— *Donald Ross*

DONALD JAMES ROSS

Born: 1872 in Dornoch, Scotland
Died: 1948 in Pinehurst, North Carolina
Career Summary
Grew up playing Dornoch and became fascinated by all aspects of golf
Served an apprenticeship at St. Andrews under Old Tom Morris
Returned to Dornoch and became course greenkeeper and also worked as a clubmaker
Emigrated to America in 1899 and became pro and greenkeeper at Oakley Golf Club in Boston
In 1901 remodeled and added nine holes to Pinehurst Resort for the Tufts family
Made many contacts at Pinehurst to design other courses, eventually started his own practice
Designed or remodeled nearly 400 courses, including some of America's most famous
Founding member of the American Society of Golf Course Architects, honorary president 1947-48

Other Interests
Rose hybridizing, turfgrass experimentation, golf club design

Published Writings
Golf Has Never Failed Me (missing commentaries eventually published in 1995)

Career Influences
The Old Course at St. Andrews, Old Tom Morris, John Sutherland, Dornoch

Golfing Ability
Professional who won two Massachusetts Opens, finished in the top 10 four times in the U.S. Open and eighth in the 1910 British Open.

Methodology
Held a winter office in Pinehurst, a summer office first in Massachusetts and later in Rhode Island as well as three branch offices. From these locations, Ross would travel to sites and design courses based on visits. During his busiest years, Ross employed many associates who would oversee construction and implementation of Ross' detailed drawings. For Northeast U.S. designs and Pinehurst, Ross was more personally involved.

Design Characteristics
Routings always took full advantage of best natural site features. First to advocate and create naturalness in construction of courses. Went through many style phases that often reflected the era when his courses were built. Green contours bold and creative. Bunkering varied in style from grass-faced to sand-faced. Was not afraid to incorporate cross-bunkers despite disapproval of poorer players.

Best Original Designs
Pinehurst Resort #2 (1903-1948)
Brae Burn Country Club (1912)
Wannamoisett Golf Club (1914)
Scioto (1916)
Oakland Hills (1917)
Interlachen (1919)
Inverness Golf Club (1920)
Oak Hill (1923, 36 holes)
Salem Country Club (1925)
Franklin Hills Country Club (1926)
Seminole (1929)

Quote
"When I was a young man in Scotland, I read about America and the American businessman absorbed in making money. I knew the day would come when the American businessman would relax and want some game to play, and I knew that game would be golf. I read about the start of golf in the United States, and knew there would be a great future in it, so I learned all I could about the game: teaching, playing, club-making, greenkeeping and course construction. And then I came to America to grow up with a game in which I had complete confidence. Golf has never failed me."

129

Second Hole at Brae Burn Country Club, West Newton, Massachusetts, Par-4, 300 Yards
"A country which gets golf-minded need not worry about the honor, the integrity and the honesty of its people."
— *Donald Ross*

Third Hole at Wannamoisett Country Club, Rumford, Rhode Island, Par-3, 135 Yards
One of Donald Ross' finest designs is at Wannamoisett. The falloff to the right of the green is reminiscent of Royal Dornoch's sixth hole.

"Putting greens constructed with relation to the length and topography of the hole are the making of a real golf course."
— Donald Ross

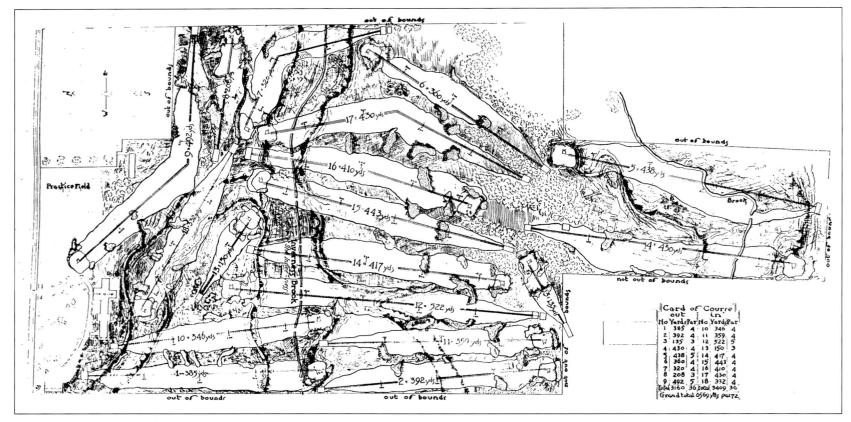

Ross Map of Inverness Club, Toledo, Ohio

"The desirable length for a good course is from 6,000 to 6,400 yards. But bear in mind that it is quality, not quantity, that counts. In my work I repeatedly have had trouble making committees see the force of this. They seem possessed with the idea that length is the main desideratum. It is beyond all argument that many a long course is noticeably uninteresting, in contrast to shorter ones that are well thought-out and skillfully constructed."

— *Donald Ross*

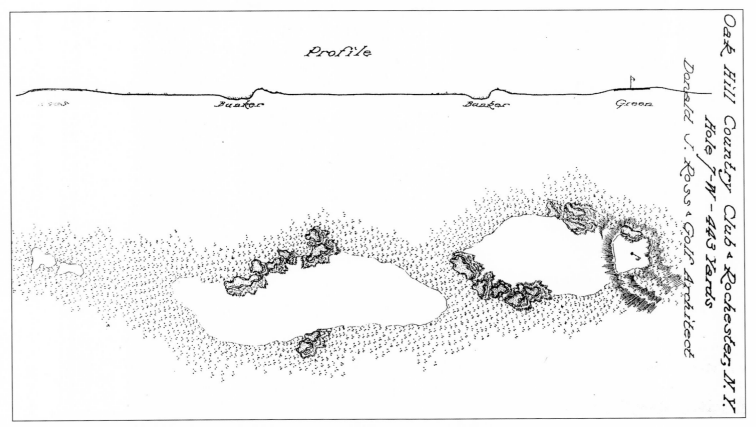

Profile

Banker   *Banker*   *Green*

Oak Hill Country Club · Rochester, N.Y.
Hole 7-W - 443 Yards
Donald J. Ross · Golf Architect

133

Ross Drawing of the Seventh Hole, Oak Hill Golf Club, Rochester, New York, Par-4, 443 Yards

"These are my standards to laying out a golf course: Make each hole present a different problem. So arrange it that every stroke must be made with a full concentration and attention necessary to good golf. Build each hole in such a manner that it wastes none of the ground at my disposal, and takes full advantage of every possibility I see."

— Donald Ross

134

**Fifth Hole at Seminole Golf Club, Palm Beach,
Florida, Par-3, 183 Yards**

*Ross used a different style of bunkering at Seminole,
with capes and bays and sand flashed in the faces.
There has long been a misconception that Dick
Wilson was responsible for this look at Seminole,
but this photo from the 1920s clearly shows that it
was an intended look from the beginning.*

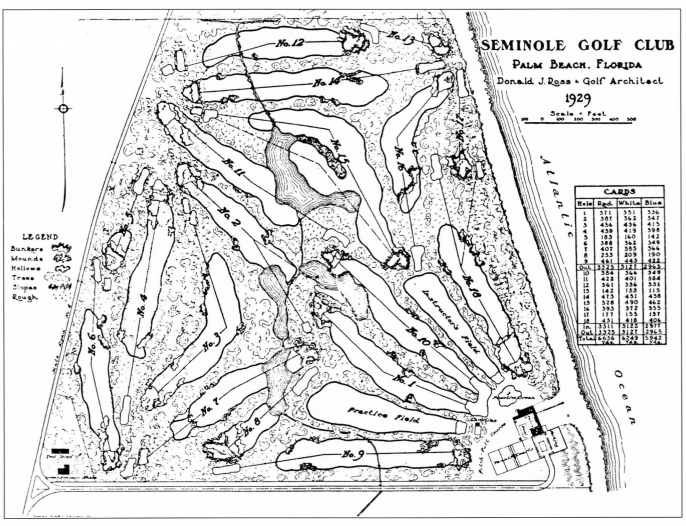

Donald Ross Drawing of Seminole in Palm Beach, Florida
"I don't say it is the best I have ever designed. Nevertheless, I like it very much."
— *Donald Ross*

135

CHAPTER FIVE

THE MACKENZIE SCHOOL of DESIGN

Although the most appropriate designation for Alister MacKenzie would have been in a design school created by his first mentor, H.S. Colt, MacKenzie's remarkable portfolio requires the designation of his own school. From masterpieces like Cypress Point and Augusta National, to lesser-known but equally as brilliant designs like Pasatiempo and Crystal Downs, MacKenzie was arguably the most charismatic, original and creative golf architect of the Golden Age.

Born in Yorkshire, England in 1870, MacKenzie spent many of his summers as a young man in the highlands of Scotland. He studied at Cambridge and earned degrees in medicine, natural science, and chemistry before serving as a field surgeon in the Boer War where he developed many of his theories on camouflage. MacKenzie studied how the Boer soldiers hid themselves in the treeless fields and later applied his observations to golf course design.

Following the war, MacKenzie briefly practiced medicine in Leeds, England, and in his spare time created models of greens and bunkers while serving as Green Committee Chairman at Alwoodley Golf Club. H.S. Colt, an established architect at the time, visited the Leeds area in 1907 and stayed at MacKenzie's residence where the two evidently discovered many philosophic similarities. Colt then requested MacKenzie's assistance in the redesign of Alwoodley. They eventually worked together on several other projects and in 1914 MacKenzie achieved some fame when his submission of a par-4 drawing won first prize in C.B. Macdonald's *Country Life* magazine contest. The contest-winning hole, judged by Horace Hutchinson, Herbert Fowler, and Bernard Darwin, was later constructed by C.B. Macdonald and Seth Raynor at the now defunct Lido Golf Club on Long Island, New York.

MacKenzie's medical practice had been dissolved and he was dabbling in architecture, but war broke out and the British Army called on his services. After the war, MacKenzie formed a partnership with Colt and C.H. Alison. Just two years later, Dr. MacKenzie published his first book, *Golf Architecture*, a concise text which was one of the first to clarify the fundamentals of design.

The Colt-MacKenzie partnership deteriorated around this time and MacKenzie began to work independently. During the 1920s MacKenzie made an extended trip through South Africa, New Zealand, and Australia, designing courses on paper and leaving them to the talented Alex Russell and others to construct. Two Australian courses, Royal Melbourne's West Course and the highly touted redesign of Kingston Heath, are the most noted layouts from this period of MacKenzie's work.

Doctor Alister MacKenzie

The late '20s marked MacKenzie's most influential accomplishments in America, where he formed three notable, but brief, design partnerships. The first was with millionaire Socialist Robert Hunter, which dissolved sometime after Cypress Point was completed. MacKenzie then joined forces with H. Chandler Egan, who was fresh off a redesign of Pebble Beach Golf Links where MacKenzie had rebuilt the eighth and thirteenth greens in 1926. But that partnership created few if any designs together. Finally, MacKenzie established a Midwest partnership with Perry Maxwell. Among his finer courses in America were his collaborations with Hunter at the Valley Club of Montecito, The Meadow Club and Cypress Point, all opened by 1928. He followed those with a solo design at his new Santa Cruz home, Pasatiempo, in 1929. He was also responsible for several other interesting California designs at Union League Golf Club, Haggin Oaks Golf Course, Claremont Country Club and Sharp Park Municipal, and redesigns at Lake Merced Golf Club and California Golf Club.

MacKenzie won the design job for Augusta National Golf Club (over a disappointed Donald Ross) sometime in late 1930 and began the two-year design process. In 1933 he completed Crystal Downs Country Club in Michigan where Perry Maxwell oversaw the construction. MacKenzie also designed the University of Michigan golf course, again supervised by Maxwell, and made plans for the Ohio State courses which were built many years after his death.

MacKenzie died in Santa Cruz, California in 1934, and his ashes were spread over the Pasatiempo golf course via airplane. Living those final years in Santa Cruz beside the sixth fairway, MacKenzie wrote a second book on architecture, *The Spirit of St. Andrews*, a manuscript thought lost until almost sixty years later when his step-grandson discovered it buried in a chest full of papers. Its brilliant content serves as a perfect reminder as to why MacKenzie may have been the most complete of all the Golden Age architects.

Second Hole at Headingly Golf Club, Leeds, England, Par-4, 400 Yards
Dr. MacKenzie's first solo design was a bit more primitive aesthetically than his later work in America.

Eighteenth Hole at Sitwell Park, England, Par-3, 140 Yards
The famous shelved green by MacKenzie in England.

"I always attempt not only to make every hole different on a golf course, but never conspicuously to reproduce two exactly similar holes. I attempt to get inspirations by seizing on any natural features and accentuating the best golfing points on them."
— *Alister MacKenzie*

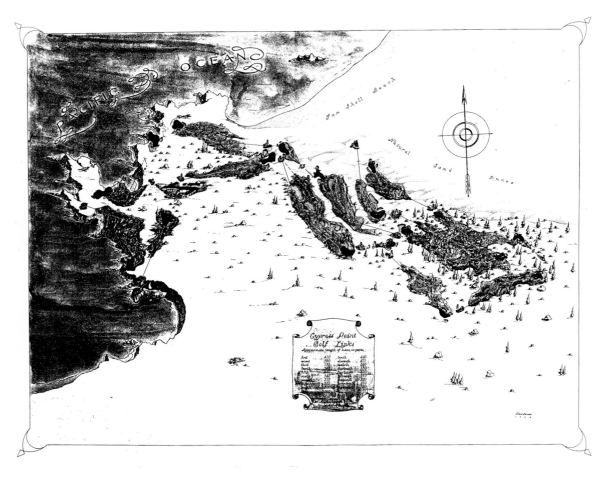

Map of Dr. MacKenzie's Initial Rendering of Cypress Point, 1928

This rendering shows his design before several major changes. In this version, the fifth is a par-4, the sixth is a par-3, and the seventh a par-4. Today those holes play as a par-5, a par-5 and a par-3. The ninth tee location is different than the final location, and the twelfth is played as a par-5 here. It was later shortened to a par-4. The thirteenth is also now a par-4, though this rendering shows it as a par-3. Another significant difference is the presence of an optional par-4 tee on the sixteenth hole which was later shortened into a one-shotter. Also note the location of the eighteenth tee, out on the cliffs. Dr. MacKenzie had thoughts of adding a tee on the small island of rocks as late as 1931. Drawings were made, but the plans were never carried out.

Second Green at Cypress Point Golf Club, Pebble Beach, California, Par-5, 548 Yards
Dr. MacKenzie is the player attempting to recover from the greenside bunker.

"A good golf course is like good music or good anything else: it is not necessarily a course which appeals the first time one plays it, but one which grows on the player the more frequently he visits it."

— *Alister MacKenzie*

Third Green at Cypress Point Golf Club, Pebble Beach, California, Par-3, 162 Yards
An artistically bunkered one-shotter, seen here just before the course opened.

"A first class architect attempts to give the impression that everything has been done by nature and nothing by himself, whereas a contractor tries to make as big a splash as possible and impress committees with the amount of labor and material he has put into the job."

— *Alister MacKenzie*

Fifth Hole at Cypress Point Golf Club, Pebble Beach, California, Par-5, 493 Yards
Dr. MacKenzie is seen here walking just beyond the primary landing area. The lay-up shot for those unable to go for the green is just past the large bunkers in the foreground.

144

Eighth Hole at Cypress Point Golf Club, Pebble Beach, California, Par-4, 363 Yards
The approach shot to the par-4 eighth plays uphill through sand dunes.

"Anything stereotyped should be avoided on a golf course; all construction work should follow the irregular lines of nature. Any contractor who informs a committee that golf courses can be constructed on contract as they would build a clubhouse is either absolutely ignorant of golf course architecture or is trying to hoodwink the golfing public. It would be just as reasonable to expect an artist to estimate the amount he charges for a painting, according to the quantities of paint and materials he uses."
— *Alister MacKenzie*

Site for the Ninth Hole at Cypress Point Golf Club, Pebble Beach, California
The dunes before construction.

146

Ninth Green at Cypress Point Golf Club, Pebble Beach, California, Par-4, 292 Yards
The ninth became a two-level putting surface cut out of the existing dunes.

Tenth Hole at Cypress Point Golf Club, Pebble Beach, California, Par-5, 480 Yards
"This axiom that no bunker is unfair wherever it is placed is the guiding principle of all golf architects…Some of us would even go further, and say that no hole is a good one unless it has one or more hazards in a direct line of a hole. Max Behr, who is one of the best American golf architects, states that the direct line to the hole is the line of instinct, and that to make a good hole you must break up that line in order to create the line of charm."

— *Alister MacKenzie*

148

Twelfth Green at Cypress Point Golf Club, Pebble Beach, California, Par-4, 404 Yards
Dr. MacKenzie putts on the twelfth green. The par-4 thirteenth hole in the distance looks like it has been there forever.

"I have not the slightest hesitation in saying that beauty means a great deal on a golf course; even the man who emphatically states that he does not care a hang for beauty is subconsciously influenced by his surroundings. A beautiful hole appeals not only to the short but also to the long handicap player, and there are few first rate holes which are not at the same time, either in the grandeur of their undulations and hazards, or the character of their surroundings, things of beauty in themselves."
— *Alister MacKenzie*

Thirteenth Hole at Cypress Point Golf Club, Pebble Beach, California, Par-4, 365 Yards
The approach to the thirteenth green is set among dunes and man-made bunkers, though it is hard to tell.

"There are few problems more difficult to solve than the problem of what actually constitutes an ideal links or an ideal hole, but it is comparatively safe to say that the ideal hole is one that affords the greatest pleasure to the greatest number, gives the fullest advantage for accurate play, stimulates players to improve their game, and which never becomes monotonous."

— Alister MacKenzie

150

Fifteenth Hole at Cypress Point Golf Club, Pebble Beach, California, Par-3, 140 Yards
One of the most stunning holes in the world, seen here before the course opened for play.

"The rock bottom test of an ideal golf course or hole is not one that enjoys a temporary popularity, but one that lives."
— *Alister MacKenzie*

Seventeenth Hole at Cypress Point Golf Club, Pebble Beach, California, Par-4, 393 Yards

A view from the tee in the early days. Originally, two options were provided from the tee. Play left of the clump of cypress trees, leaving a longer shot to the well-trapped green. Or, the player could place their drive close to the bunkers in front of the cypress trees, leaving a shorter shot to the green. A championship tee above one of the rear bunkers on the sixteenth once stretched the hole to 410 yards.

</>

ROBERT HUNTER

(*1874-1942*)

One of the most fascinating characters in early twentieth century golf architecture, Robert Hunter designed only one golf course on his own. Besides his lone but brilliant book on golf architecture, *The Links*, Hunter was a best-selling writer of numerous books dealing with social ills. He had even run for public office in Connecticut as a Socialist. More remarkably, Hunter was a multimillionaire when he was in the midst of his Socialist campaigning.

Hunter's golf course architecture career was limited to assisting Dr. Alister MacKenzie on such noted California courses as Cypress Point Club, The Meadow Club, and The Valley Club of Montecito, and one solo design in Berkeley, California. A native of Indiana, Hunter also contributed to some minor redesign work at Monterey Peninsula Country Club's underrated Dunes Course and was on the committee with H. Chandler Egan redesigning Pebble Beach Golf Links in 1928.

The depth of *The Links* might persuade even a beginning student of golf course architecture that Hunter significantly shaped MacKenzie's philosophy. To learn otherwise, however, all one has to do is read MacKenzie's 1920 book, *Golf Architecture,* which is a concise explanation of architecture, and his 1934 manuscript *The Spirit of St. Andrews*, a much more profound and refined book on the subject. In between the publication of those books, MacKenzie was exposed to many interesting thinkers, including Hunter. But Robert Hunter's greatest influence on MacKenzie surely came at Cypress Point where, with the help of Marion Hollins, the three crafted what many call the most "perfect" golf course design man has ever seen.

"In the design and construction of Cypress Point I was fortunate in being associated with Mr. Robert Hunter, the author of The Links, *which is by far the best book on golf architecture ever written."*

— *Alister MacKenzie*

152

MARION HOLLINS
(1892-1944)

One of America's finest female players in the first half of the twentieth century, Marion Hollins was also a major figure in golf architecture circles and the driving force behind two of Alister MacKenzie's finest designs, Cypress Point and Pasatiempo.

A Long Island native, Hollins won the U.S. Amateur in 1921 and soon after, founded, built, and managed the Women's National Golf Club in New York. She later moved to Pebble Beach to serve as the "athletic director" at Pebble Beach. After a short time there, Samuel Morse put Hollins in charge of the new Cypress Point development where she organized the membership and hired Dr. Alister MacKenzie to design the golf course.

By that time, Hollins had amassed a large fortune and turned her focus to the creation of Pasatiempo in Santa Cruz. Besides hiring MacKenzie, Hollins also employed the famous Olmsted Brothers firm (Central Park) to create the master development plan that included tennis, polo facilities and numerous homesites along the golf course.

Regarding the famous par-3 sixteenth hole at Cypress Point, Alister MacKenzie had this to say in his book *The Spirit of St. Andrews*: "To give honor where it is due, I must say that, except for minor details in construction, I was in no way responsible for the hole. It was largely due to the vision of Miss Marion Hollins (the founder of Cypress Point). It was suggested to her by the late Seth Raynor that it was a pity the carry over the ocean was too long to enable a hole to be designed on this particular site. Miss Hollins said she did not think it was an impossible carry. She then teed up a ball and drove to the middle of the site for the suggested green."

"The formation of Cypress Point was due to the energy and foresight of Miss Marion Hollins. Miss Hollins has a flair for discovering ideal golfing sites. She was the founder of the American Women's National and has recently discovered a magnificent site for a golf course at Santa Cruz, which will doubtless increase the popularity of Santa Cruz as a seaside resort."

— *Alister MacKenzie*

153

154

Sixteenth Hole at Cypress Point Golf Club, Pebble Beach, California, Par-3, 235 Yards
View from the clubhouse patio of MacKenzie's most famous par-3. The tee is out of view on the right.

"The desirability or otherwise of having water hazards depends largely on their spectacular character and beauty. The amazing thrill of driving successfully over the ocean at the sixteenth hole at Cypress Point more than compensates for the loss of a dozen balls. Even absolute dubs succumb to this thrill."
— *Alister MacKenzie*

Eighteenth Hole at Cypress Point Golf Club, Pebble Beach, California, Par-4, 345 Yards
The view from the tee on the eighteenth, a hole that has come under attack as a poor finishing hole. In Dr. MacKenzie's version, bunkers shaped the tee shot so much so that the fairway was almost completely surrounded by sand. The overhanging trees were also a factor, making it a most difficult finishing hole. At one point, consideration was given to building a tee out in the ocean atop a set of large rocks. Extensive plans were made for a bridge to the rocks, but the plan was never carried out.

ROBERT TYRE JONES, JR. *(1902-1971)*

Though he never practiced architecture, Bobby Jones hired and worked with Alister MacKenzie on the original design of Augusta National, and later with Robert Trent Jones on the Peachtree Golf Club in Atlanta. He never professed to be an architect, but Jones' influence on these famed courses along with his writings earns him a special place amongst the figures from the Golden Age of Golf Design.

Jones and MacKenzie have long been presumed to have met after Jones' abrupt departure from the first round of the 1929 U.S. Amateur at Pebble Beach. Jones did play an exhibition with Francis Ouimet and others at Cypress Point after his U.S. Amateur loss. And he did play Pasatiempo on opening day where MacKenzie was in the gallery, but the two had met several years before at St. Andrews. MacKenzie was present for many of Jones' competitive rounds on the Old Course and he talked of knowing Jones long before they supposedly met in 1929. However, there is little question that the stunning nature of MacKenzie's designs at Cypress Point and Pasatiempo was the deciding factor for the Augusta National commission.

The strategic design of Augusta has been and always will be its finest attribute, and MacKenzie himself was adamant about Jones' influence on the original layout. It's doubtful that MacKenzie could have pulled off the very un-American look of roughless fairways, bold green contours, and a select number of bunkers if it weren't for Jones' influence. Particularly with the meddlesome Clifford Roberts running the show and obsessing over every detail.

Bobby Jones also helped design the par-3 course at Augusta with George Cobb. (MacKenzie reportedly laid out an 18-hole version in the initial planning stages. It is not known if any of his design was used for the course.) Jones' endorsement of "short courses" helped start a nationwide boom in par-3 course construction during the 1950s and '60s. Jones was also a prolific and often times poetic writer who frequently commented on architecture when few others dared to touch the subject.

In his Foreword to MacKenzie's *The Spirit of St. Andrews*, Jones eloquently summarized why it is important for all golfers to understand at least the basic principles of course design. He wrote, "Every golfer worthy of the name should have some acquaintance with the principles of golf course design, not only for the betterment of the game, but for his own selfish enjoyment. Let him know a good hole from a bad one and the reasons for a bunker here and another there, and he will be a long way towards pulling his score down to respectable limits. When he has taught himself to study a hole from the point of view of the man who laid it out, he will be much more likely to play it correctly."

Eighth Green at Pasatiempo Golf Club, Santa Cruz, California, Par-3, 175 Yards
The downhill, severely sloped eighth green at Pasatiempo is in the foreground, with the par-5 ninth in the distance.

"I have always wanted to live where one could practice shots in one's pajamas before breakfast, and at Santa Cruz the climate is so delightful that one can play golf every day in the year, where it is never too hot and never too cold, and if it should rain it usually does so at night."

— Alister MacKenzie

Thirteenth Green at Pasatiempo Golf Club, Santa Cruz, California, Par-5, 492 Yards
An artistically bunkered three-shotter with Dr. MacKenzie's handwritten description.

Pasatiempo
Santa Cruz

13ᵗʰ Green
A three shot-hole

Eighteenth Hole at Pasatiempo Golf Club, Santa Cruz, California, Par-3, 175 Yards
The downhill finishing hole at Dr. MacKenzie's final home course, with his handwritten description.

160

Seventh Green at Lake Merced Golf Club, San Francisco, California, Par-4, 444 Yards
A course remodeled by Dr. MacKenzie but subsequently changed.

Eighth Green at Lake Merced Golf Club, San Francisco, California, Par-3, 165 Yards
Spectacular bunkering makes this hole one of the most memorable par-3s MacKenzie ever designed. According to John Fleming, whose father Jack was one of Dr. MacKenzie's associates for many years, MacKenzie's crews shaped the bunkers to resemble the look of irregularly shaped floating clouds. Fleming learned of this style as a boy spending time with one of the crews. The lead bunker shaper was an Irishman named Paddy Cole who shared his "secret" method to creating such artistic bunkers.

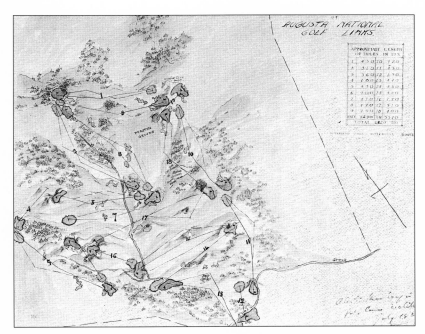

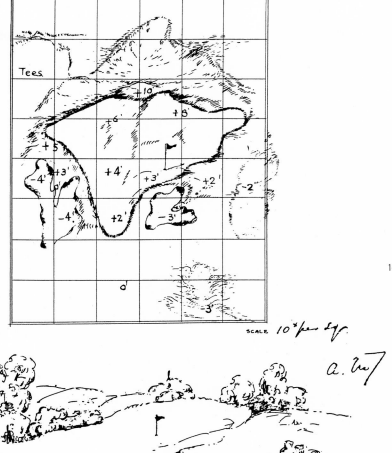

Dr. MacKenzie's Initial Routing of Augusta National Golf Club, July 1931
A watercolor rendering of Augusta with the nines in today's order. Note the use of intersected lines to imply the many alternate routes available on certain holes.

Dr. MacKenzie's Diagram for the Fourth Green at Augusta National Golf Club, an Adaptation of the Eden Hole on the Old Course at St. Andrews.
"There is no hole that has been copied more frequently than the eleventh at St. Andrews, but I do not know any copy that has the charm, the interest, or the thrills of the original. This is largely owing to the fact that the subtle slopes of the green and approach are overlooked, and there are few, if any, architects who have the courage to give the same marked tilt to the green, being much too afraid of hostile criticism. An architect fears the cry of freakishness, and the uproar of the press, if perchance, some popular competitor like Bobby Jones putts a little too strongly and his ball rushes down the steep slope into Strath bunker, which is not an infrequent occurrence at this hole."
— Alister MacKenzie

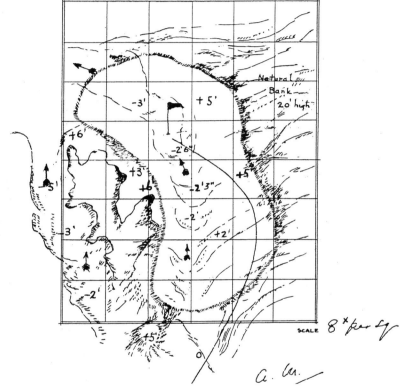

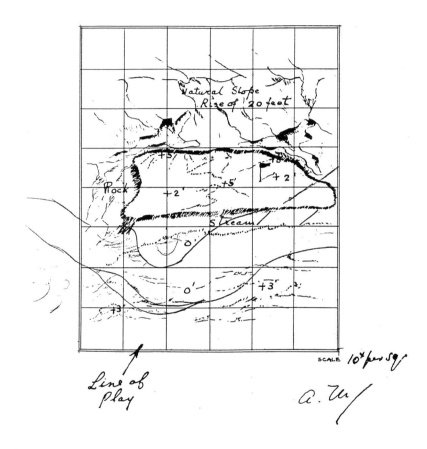

Dr. MacKenzie's Diagram for the Tenth Green at Augusta National Golf Club.
The green was originally situated near the large bunker which now serves as a cross-bunker for a 485-yard hole today. Perry Maxwell relocated the tenth hole green location in 1937.

Dr. MacKenzie's Diagram for the Twelfth Green at Augusta National Golf Club.
The green was originally much larger with more undulation than today's version.

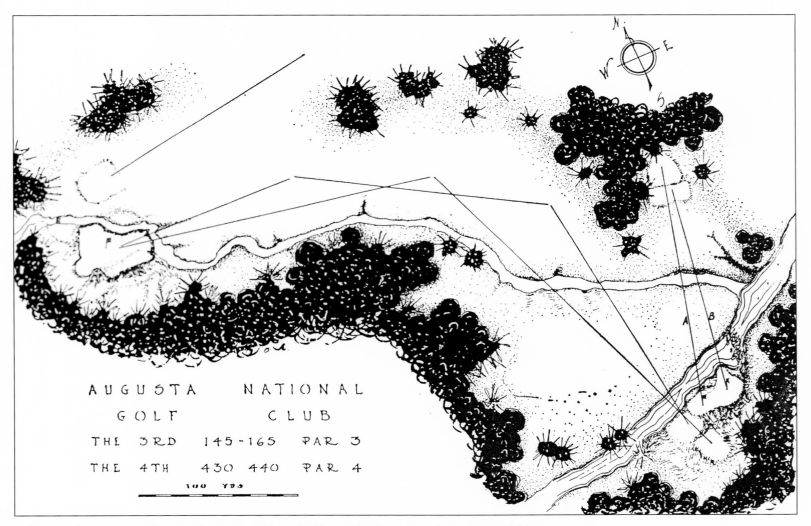

AUGUSTA   NATIONAL
GOLF   CLUB
THE 3RD   145-165 PAR 3
THE 4TH   430 440 PAR 4
100 YDS

Dr. MacKenzie's Overhead Drawing for the Twelfth and Thirteenth Holes at Augusta National Golf Club.
In this pre-opening day version, the famed thirteenth is referred to as the fourth and was designed as a par-4. Dr. MacKenzie wisely lengthened it into a short par-5 before the course opened for play and it remains today as the most tempting, seductive, and ideal three-shotter in golf.

164

Thirteenth Green at Augusta National Golf Club, Augusta, Georgia, Par-5, 445 Yards (Original Yardage)
The famed thirteenth green is seen here before the course opened.

"There are two ways of widening the gap between the good tee shot and a bad one. One is to inflict punishment upon the bad shot, to place its perpetrator in a bunker or in some other trouble which will demand the sacrifice of a stroke in recovering. The other, is to reward the good shot by making the second shot simpler in proportion to the excellence of the drive. In this way, upon the long well-placed drive — possibly the one which has dared an impressive bunker — is conferred the greatest benefit; but shots of less excellence are still left with the opportunity to retrieve their fortune by bringing off an exceptionally fine second."
— *Bobby Jones*

Fourteenth Green at Augusta National Golf Club, Augusta, Georgia, Par-4, 405 Yards
The bunkerless fourteenth green at Augusta, which plays similarly today.

"Today nearly everyone plays a coarse and vulgar pitch which punches a hole in the green. With the exception of the Old Course at St. Andrews and few similar courses, there is rarely any necessity to play any other kind of shot. Golfers are losing the joy of playing the variety of approach shots that were so necessary in the old days."
— Alister MacKenzie

166

Sixteenth Green at Augusta National Golf Club, Augusta, Georgia, Par-3, 145 Yards
This hole was removed because it was perceived as being too short. The current sixteenth green sits on the opposite side of the creek that fronts the old green.

"The difference between the golf courses of America and Great Britain can best be expressed by the two words 'artificial' and 'natural,' and that means a whole lot more than the mere presence or absence of the fabrication of man."

— Bobby Jones

DR. ALEXANDER "ALI/TER" MACKENZIE

Born: August 30, 1870 in Yorkshire, England
Died: January 6, 1934 in Santa Cruz, California
Career Summary
Raised in Scottish Highlands, received Bachelor of Medicine and Surgery from Cambridge in 1897
Served as Alwoodley Green Chairman in early 1900s, worked with H.S. Colt in redesigning course
Dissolved brief medical practice soon thereafter and joined Colt in architecture practice
Won First Prize in 1914 *Country Life* magazine design contest
Served as physician during Boer War and World War I
Credited with saving thousands of lives during wars thanks to implementation of his camouflage theories
Created own practice during 1920s and traveled the world, establishing him as a renowned architect
Moved to California in late '20s and constructed several world famous courses, including Cypress Point
Died in 1934 before publication of his second book, *The Spirit of St. Andrews*

Other Interests
General medicine practice, military camouflage, gardening and landscape architecture, dancing
Published Writings
Golf Architecture (1920)
The Spirit of St. Andrews (completed in 1934, published 1995)
Numerous magazine articles on golf architecture, maintenance, and military camouflage
Career Influences
The Old Course at St. Andrews, Old Tom Morris, H.S. Colt, military camouflage, English landscape architects Capability Brown and Humphrey Repton, bunker shaper Paddy Cole
Golfing Ability
Poor to average player early in life, became a more accomplished golfer in his final years at Pasatiempo thanks to teachings of Ernest Jones and Bobby Jones.

Design Characteristics
Master of strategic and playable design. Routings never followed set formula, relied on natural features to dictate order of holes. Responsible for eccentric, irregular bunker designs shaped like passing clouds. Frugal but ingenious placement of hazards. Placed many hazards to add interest for the below average players as well as low handicappers. Green contours often bold but always designed to reward those approaching from the appropriate angles.
Best Original Design Work
Alwoodley Golf Club (1907 with H.S. Colt)
Royal Adelaide Golf Club (1926 redesign)
Royal Melbourne Golf Club—West Course (1931, with Alex Russell)
Kingston Heath Golf Club (1928 redesign with Alex Russell)
Cypress Point Golf Club (1928 with Robert Hunter

and Marion Hollins)
The Valley Club of Montecito (1928 with Robert Hunter)
Pasatiempo Golf Club (1929 with Marion Hollins)
Augusta National Golf Club (1933 with Bobby Jones)
Crystal Downs Country Club (1933 with Perry Maxwell)
Quote
"...golf is a game and not a mathematical business, and that it is of vital importance to avoid anything that tends to make the game simple and stereotyped. On the contrary, every endeavor should be made to increase its strategy, variety, mystery, charm and elusiveness so that we shall never get bored with it, but continue to pursue it with increasing zest, as many of the old stalwarts of St. Andrews do, for the remainder of our lives."

167

MAX BEHR

(1884-1955)

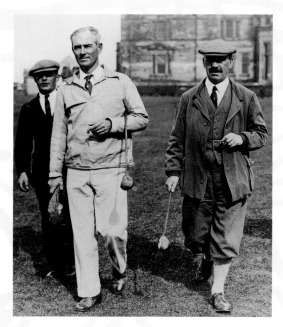

Max Behr and Dr. MacKenzie

Not only did the Golden Age rely on notable architects, but also on men who "spread the word" and who took the initiative to educate golfers. Early on there was Bernard Darwin in England and Walter Travis in America. However, in 1914 Max Behr became editor of *Golf Illustrated* and forever changed the attitude magazines had toward golf course design.

Behr was another of the many Yale graduates who played the game proficiently and who became fascinated with golf architecture. He had a fine amateur record, highlighted by a final match loss in the 1908 U.S. Amateur to Jerome Travers. After slowing down his competitive career, Behr took the job as Editor of *Golf Illustrated* in 1914 where he expanded the new magazine's coverage to all facets of the game, with an emphasis on rules and architecture. As can be seen by the many photographs in this book courtesy of *Golf Illustrated*, the magazine featured numerous photographs and frequent commentary on golf course design, with Behr doing much of the writing himself.

In 1918 his first wife died suddenly, and a heartbroken Behr moved to California to start his life over. It was there he refined his ideas on design, constructed several fine layouts, and played a role in the career of Alister MacKenzie. In California he joined George Thomas, Billy Bell, Norman MacBeth and Willie Watson as a practicing architect in the fast-growing region. Though MacKenzie called Behr's Lakeside design "one of the world's greatest golf courses," it was Behr's ability to write and defend the cause of strategic design that made his contributions to golf architecture unforgettable. He continued writing for various publications upon arriving out West, and though he could be a bit fanatical at times, it was Behr's passion for the subject and his analogies to classic art that opened many golfer's eyes to the intricacies and possibilities in golf course design. Many of his writings on strategy and the need for architects to break up "the line of charm" were repeated in slightly different form by MacKenzie in *The Spirit of St. Andrews*.

At Lakeside, Behr featured man-made dunes on several holes and also designed wide fairways and strategically bunkered greens to model the style of the Old Course at St. Andrews. The course may have been a bit ahead of its time, as it was not as widely praised as other Southern California courses, but MacKenzie's endorsement says something about its worth. Other excellent Behr designs included Hacienda Country Club, Rancho Santa Fe Country Club, Victoria Golf Club and some minor consulting work on The Olympic Club's two courses.

His writings, which require a dictionary at hand but are sure to entertain, range from "The Nature and Use of Penalty" to "Art in Golf Architecture" to repeated commentaries over the years about "The Ball Problem." (His feelings varied, but he was consistently for anything that kept skill important and prevented power from overtaking the game.) Behr also engaged British golf writer Joshua Crane in a lengthy and sometimes hostile debate over the merits of strategic design versus penal design.

"Unfortunately, hazards have come to be associated with an idea of penalty...This has resulted in establishing a system of course design in which hazards are used to indicate a fixed idea of what correct play should be. To enforce this requires discipline. Thus hazards, besides being informative of what correct play should be, become agents of the discipline necessary to enforce it. And as discipline, if it is to effect obedience, must be definite and self-revealing, this system robs golf of all mystery, romance and adventure. Play becomes no more than an examination of skill. The golfer is not required to think, but merely to obey."
— *Max Behr*

168

Thirteenth Green at Lakeside Golf Club, North Hollywood, California, Par-4, 350 Yards
Alister MacKenzie considered Behr's original design at Lakeside one of the best in the world. This green was washed away permanently in the winter of 1938.

"...with something which to whet his skill and make him think, the golfer reacts vitally to the vital circumstances that confront him. He is taken out of himself. His golf becomes objective. No longer is he so given to that subjective disease, the dwelling of thought upon how he should address his ball, hold his hands, and what not. He is having too much fun."

— Max Behr

CHAPTER SIX

THE MONTEREY SCHOOL of DESIGN

Of all the various "schools" of design, the Monterey institute was certainly the smallest and least prolific. However, the impact of its primary creation, Pebble Beach Golf Links, was and continues to be a monumental design in the world of golf. Not only is Pebble Beach the most recognizable course in the world, it is one of the most shrewdly designed.

Sometime in 1915, Samuel Morse was given the task of liquidating the land holdings of the Pacific Improvement Company. One of the areas Morse was responsible for dividing up and selling was the Monterey Peninsula. But he was so enamored with the area and its potential that Morse opted to start his own company, Del Monte Properties, and purchased nearly 7,000 acres for a paltry $1.3 million.

His dream was to create a resort and real estate development built around a scenic 17-mile long road. Among the amenities planned were several golf courses to complement the already existing, but extraordinarily primitive, Del Monte Golf Course.

The original master plan, conceived by Morse's friend and Del Monte Properties employee Jack Neville, was for the golf course to meander through the inland terrain with large homesites fronting the ocean. But Morse realized that he was wasting the opportunity of a

lifetime by not putting the course along the ocean and he ordered Neville to alter the plan, with golf taking priority.

As a former state amateur champion with some knowledge of golf architecture, Neville was also given the task of designing the course. Morse had tried to lure C.B. Macdonald and Donald Ross to the peninsula to do the job, but each declined what turned out to be a once-in-a-lifetime opportunity. For several weeks in 1916, Jack Neville walked the site and created the famed figure eight routing. He worked with another state amateur champion, Douglas Grant, who had recently returned from Scotland and was fresh with ideas. Their design opened in 1918 and was criticized for its difficulty. Further refinements made the Pebble Beach course more playable for the next ten years. However, when Roger Lapham convinced the United States Golf Association to bring the 1929 U.S. Amateur to the West Coast, Morse green-lighted another course upgrade. Enter Chandler Egan.

Though the Neville/Grant routing was kept in place, Chandler Egan is largely responsible for the modern-day masterpiece known as Pebble Beach. Along with Lapham, course superintendent Joe Mayo and Robert Hunter, Egan rebuilt sixteen of the eighteen greens and completely reshaped the appearance and location of the bunkers. Dr.

MacKenzie, who would later hire Egan as part of his design firm, had redesigned the eighth and thirteenth holes in 1926 and Egan chose to keep those intact. It is unknown why MacKenzie did not get the job to renovate the whole course after redesigning those two greens in an apparent "tryout."

Despite all of the assistance, Chandler Egan was the visionary behind the Pebble Beach remodel. His previous design work was limited to courses in the Northwest United States, but as one of the premier amateur golfers in America, Egan garnered tremendous respect. He had traveled the world and understood the elements of strategic golf architecture.

Egan and Joe Mayo, who both supervised construction on site, also experimented with "imitation sand dunes" that can be seen in the old photographs of Pebble Beach. They immediately transformed an awkward but well-routed golf course into one of the best in the world. And even though the imitation sand dunes have been replaced with regularly edged bunkers due to time, play, and weather, Pebble Beach still retains the subtle character and strategic genius of Chandler Egan and his friends, the founders of the Monterey School of Design.

"The Monterey Peninsula was designed by nature as a great golfing center. The ocean had eaten its way into the coast and made innumerable little bays and arms of the sea. There are sandy beaches, headlands and capes covered with good turf and grass. The setting offered a wonderful opportunity for the genius of the architect."

— *Samuel Morse*

172

Seventh Green at Pebble Beach Prior to 1928 Renovation

The larger, more regularly shaped seventh green prior to Chandler Egan's dramatic 1928 redesign of the course. Egan kept the tee and green locations the same, but dramatically altered the surrounding bunkers. See page 180 for the Egan version.

SAMUEL MORSE

(1886-1969)

Named after his distant relative and inventor of the telegraph, Samuel Morse not only created the Pebble Beach resort community but he fostered it until his death in 1969. A 1907 graduate of Yale where he captained the football team, Morse was given the task of liquidating the Pacific Improvement Company's unprofitable "Del Monte unit."

Instead, he decided to buy the Del Monte unit but was surprisingly turned down for financing by longtime friend and Yale classmate Templeton Crocker, who viewed the loan as a conflict of interest. Finally, he found a taker in Anglo Bank president Herbert Fleishhacker. Anglo financed the purchase after becoming a partner in the new Del Monte Properties Company. Morse took over management of the existing lodge and land when the Del Monte Properties Company was formed and the thirty-three year old Morse began implementing his plans for a world-class resort.

An avid cartoonist and extremely creative man, Samuel Morse made this observation of the existing and primitive Del Monte Golf Course:

"There were extraordinary little mounds called 'chocolate drops,' a type of hazard I had never seen on any other course. They were situated to the right of the first fairway and the bunkers were in a straight line across the fairway. The whole course looked as though it had been laid out with a ruler and there had been no effort to make it conform to the natural contours of the ground."

Morse did not make the same mistake in the construction of what was originally known as Del Monte's Second Course and later changed to Pebble Beach. Despite the excellent work of Jack Neville, Douglas Grant, Alister MacKenzie, Chandler Egan, Robert Hunter and others, it was Morse who had the instinct to hire these talented architects and give them free rein.

Samuel Morse made an even more unprecedented hiring in 1926, giving Marion Hollins the chance to create and operate the Del Monte Properties new Cypress Point development. And we all know how well that turned out.

173

JACK NEVILLE & DOUGLAS GRANT

Jack Neville

A real estate salesman by trade, Jack Neville was asked to design Pebble Beach in 1915 by Samuel Morse. Neville had captured the California State Amateur in 1912 and 1913 and was considered one of the finest amateurs in America. Besides having C.B. Macdonald and Donald Ross decline the opportunity, few other practicing architects were available for the Pebble Beach job because of World War I. With the common perception then that playing ability equaled design talent, Neville became a natural choice to design Samuel Morse's new Del Monte Golf Links.

Neville, in turn, asked his friend Douglas Grant, also a former California Amateur Champion to assist in the design. When completed in 1918, the Neville and Grant design measured a little over 6,300 yards and played to a par of 74. Though Chandler Egan completely changed the style and placement of the greens and hazards and made many other significant changes, it is Neville and Grant's original figure eight routing that gives Pebble Beach so much of its unique character.

Many architects might have just sent the first nine holes inland through the Monterey cypress and swung the course back in along the cliffs of the Pacific Ocean, creating what surely would have been a dramatic finishing nine. However, Neville and Grant opted to tease the golfer with a stretch of holes bordering the Pacific in the middle of the round, before heading inland until the dramatic seventeenth and eighteenth holes reemerge along the coast. This divergent set of holes, which provided a balance of different looks and took better advantage of the terrain, makes the routing of Pebble Beach both unique and remarkable considering it came from two "amateurs."

Neville was involved in other projects including a 1961 co-design with Bob Baldock on the Monterey Peninsula Country Club's Shore Course, the addition of nine holes to the charming Pacific Grove Municipal Course, and some consultation on George Thomas and Billy Bell's Bel-Air Country Club design in Los Angeles. He was also consulted by Sandy Tatum on minor course changes prior to the 1972 U.S. Open at Pebble Beach. Neville was instrumental in spreading the word on early California golf courses as the editor of *Pacific Golf and Motor Magazine*. Grant, on the other hand, was not involved in any other designs except for some consulting at Pebble Beach in the early years after the course opened.

H. CHANDLER EGAN

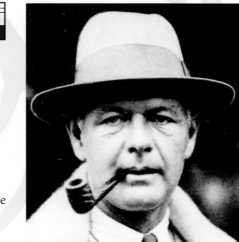

Born: 1884 in Chicago, Illinois
Died: 1936 in Everett, Washington
Golf Career Summary
1902 NCAA Individual Golf Champion playing for Harvard
1904 and 1905 United States Amateur Champion
4-time Western Amateur Champion
Semi-finalist in 1929 U.S. Amateur at Pebble Beach at age of 45

Design Career Summary
Graduate of Harvard University, 1905
Established golf architecture business in 1910
Designed courses primarily in Northwest United States
Hired as head of a "committee of three" to remodel Pebble Beach prior to 1929 U.S. Amateur
Joined Alister MacKenzie design firm in 1929, representing MacKenzie in the Western U.S.

Published Writings
Various articles in regional golf magazines previewing changes made to Pebble Beach in 1928-29. Also wrote instruction articles and essays on golf.

Career Influences
The Old Course at St. Andrews, Alister MacKenzie, and virtually all important early American and Scottish architecture seen as a tournament contestant.

Design Characteristics
Believed in simple strategic problems created by bunkering schemes and angles of green design. Created multiple options of play on many holes. Emphasized natural, irregular bunkering. Greens medium in size with steep pitches dictating hole strategy.

Best Design Work
Pebble Beach Golf Links (1928, redesign with Robert Hunter and Roger Lapham)
Eugene Country Club (1926, since completely changed)
Riverside Golf and Country Club (1928, added 9)
Waverley Country Club (1930 redesign)
Pacific Grove Municipal (1932, front nine)
Green Hills Country Club (1932, with Alister MacKenzie and Hunter)

Quote
"I do not believe that there exists a lovelier situation in the world, particularly for golf, than the Monterey Peninsula. Then, too, the Pebble Beach course has always proved itself to be a fine test of golf in a hundred and one contests. There is every reason to suppose that with its recent improvements it will be an even finer proving ground for all the shots in the one hundred and sixty-two bags that will be allowed to show their mettle."

175

Breakdown of the H. Chandler Egan Remodel of Pebble Beach in 1928

#1 New tee built to add sixty yards to hole. Several bunkers added.

#2 New tees built to add thirty yards to hole. Green moved away from road and new bunkering scheme employed. Hazard in front of green brought more into play, creating forced carry.

#3 New tee adds twenty-five yards to hole and creates 205-yard carry over gully. Original green shrunken and new greenside bunkers added to reward tee shots played on riskier line of play.

#4 Tee extended twenty yards. Green rebuilt and moved closer to ocean. New "imitation sand dunes" built to completely surround green.

#5 New green moved to left closer to ravine. Three traps built.

#6 "Radical change" according to Egan. Lengthened to 500 yards but still designed as a gambling par-5 for better players. Green moved closer to cliff and back towards #7 tee. Several new bunkers added to define layup and second shots. More imitation sand dunes surrounding green constructed.

#7 Old green site rebuilt, retaining shape but eliminating geometric characteristics in favor of irregular edges. Green is "completely surrounded by sand dune bunkering."

#8 Hole lengthened by twenty-five yards, three new bunkers surrounding green installed and green edges slightly reshaped.

#9 New green built extending hole by fifty yards. Two-tier fairway created, rewarding risky tee shots played near the ocean with open view to the green.

#10 New tee built above and behind new ninth green, extending yardage. Sand trap built in fairway creating two routes of play. New green constructed and surrounded by imitation sand dunes.

#11 Fairway bunkers installed and new green constructed with bunkering designed to complement proper tee shot placement.

#12 Green rebuilt with the opening to the right instead of to the left as was the case with the old green. New bunkers added short of and next to green.

#13 Fairway bunker significantly changed to create strategic placement on tee shot. MacKenzie green kept.

#14 Green rebuilt and made smaller and sloping away in back. New trap added to guard front. Overall green complex designed to create difficult third shot.

#15 New green on old location designed to be approached from the left side of fairway. More bunkering added around green.

#16 Twenty yards added to the hole. Large diagonal sand hazard is built creating three tee shot options. Arm of gully extended in front of green.

#17 Lengthened to 225 yards. Large hourglass green with sand dune bunkering is constructed.

#18 Tee extended and rebuilt green more closely trapped to create difficulty.

176

MACKENZIE & EGAN

Golf Course Architects

OFFICE: AGNEW & BOEKEL
FEDERAL RESERVE BANK BLDG.
SAN FRANCISCO

❧

DR. A. MACKENZIE
CYPRESS POINT GOLF CLUB
PEBBLE BEACH

ASSOCIATE
F. H. BICKERTON
BOX 152-SANTA CRUZ

H. CHANDLER EGAN
PEBBLE BEACH OR
MEDFORD, OREGON

Chandler Egan joined Alister MacKenzie's design firm in the fall of 1929. It is doubtful that Dr. MacKenzie ever shared top billing with anyone else he practiced architecture with. However, Egan's work at Pebble Beach was so remarkable and nationally praised that Dr. MacKenzie surely wanted some part of that respect as well as an association with a major up-and-coming architect.

Chandler Egan Surveys the Reconstruction of Pebble Beach in 1928.
Egan reportedly hit shots to potential green sites before deciding on final designs. Once he had made up his mind, he produced miniature models. He is seen here smoking his trademark pipe with one such model in front of him.

177

Fourth Green at Pebble Beach Golf Links, Pebble Beach, California, Par-4, 325 Yards
"The green was rebuilt a little to the right and as close to the ocean as possible. It is rather small and almost completely surrounded by small imitation sand dunes. Joe Mayo and I had never seen this type of bunkering done before but we had faith in the idea and after a few experiments achieved a result that we hope will continue to be as good as it seems at this writing."

— *H. Chandler Egan*

Sixth Hole at Pebble Beach Golf Links, Pebble Beach, California, Par-5, 500 Yards
The long sixth as viewed from the tee with two bunkers situated on the hillside.

**Seventh Green at Pebble Beach Golf Links,
Pebble Beach, California, Par-3, 107 Yards**
*Two views of the famed oceanside par-3, showing
more of Chandler Egan's innovative "imitation sand
dune bunkering."*

Eighth Green at Pebble Beach Golf Links, Pebble Beach, California, Par-4, 425 Yards
Dr. Alister MacKenzie deserves credit for the design of this green along with Chandler Egan. MacKenzie redesigned the eighth and thirteenth greens in 1926 in an apparent audition for the 1928 renovation of Pebble Beach, which went to Chandler Egan instead.

The "New" #9 at Pebble Beach Golf Links, Pebble Beach, California, Par-4, 450 Yards

Joe Mayo was the Pebble Beach superintendent in the late '20s and '30s. He oversaw construction of Chandler Egan's reconstruction of Pebble Beach and documented the new holes with sketches that appeared in The National Greenkeeper. *Photograph shows the alternate fairways on the Pebble Beach ninth, with the right side fairway clearing offering a more appealing approach shot than the left fairway.*

"Here is the most radical change in all of the new work. Practically all of the old hole has been abandoned. The new tees are just back of the eighth green and the new fairway includes only the right-hand edge of the old fairway and extends to the right to the ocean edge. The new topography is very interesting and impossible to describe here. The new green is located beyond the gully that used to be in front of the old tenth tee. Thus the new hole is about forty or fifty yards longer than the old one, and has brought the element of ocean risk. There are decidedly two routes to play which the player should bear in mind as he tackles this hole."

— H. Chandler Egan

182

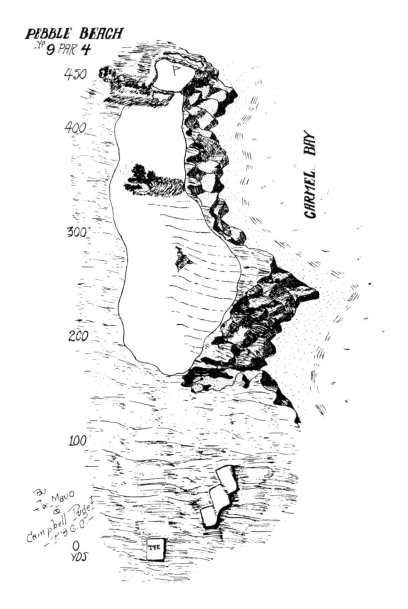

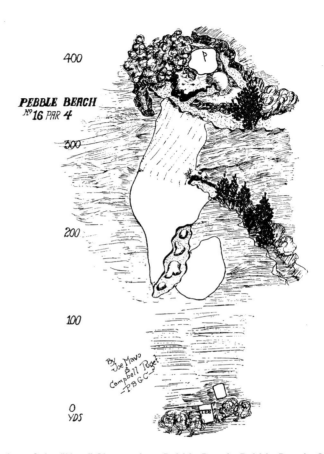

Tenth Green at Pebble Beach Golf Links, Pebble Beach, California, Par-4, 405 Yards

"A large sand trap is in the center of a wide fairway dividing the hole into two routes. The green was rebuilt as close to the ocean as possible and is guarded at the back and ocean side by sand dune bunkering. A small irregular trap at the front center of the green comes decidedly into play and may be the factor that determines your route from the tee."

— *H. Chandler Egan*

Drawing of the "New" Sixteenth at Pebble Beach, Pebble Beach, California, Par-4, 400 Yards

Pebble Beach superintendent Joe Mayo described the newly rebuilt sixteenth, one of Chandler Egan's most dramatic design changes: "A great natural golf hole with a diagonal carry of sandy badlands. The player is forced to place his tee shot as near as possible to the end of the barranca on the right which is the ideal location. A series of oak trees to the left combine to make the second shot more difficult; usually a 4-iron or more. This hole calls for distinct placing of shots and the natural trouble is serious."

Seventeenth Green, Pebble Beach Golf Links, Pebble Beach, California, Par-3, 225 Yards
Tee view of the famous seventeenth where more imitation sand dunes were constructed.

Seventeenth Green, Pebble Beach Golf Links, Pebble Beach, California, Par-3, 225 Yards
Another close-up view of the seventeenth green, showing it nearly doubled in size as compared to today's putting surface. The large yacht in the background belonged to Howard Hughes.

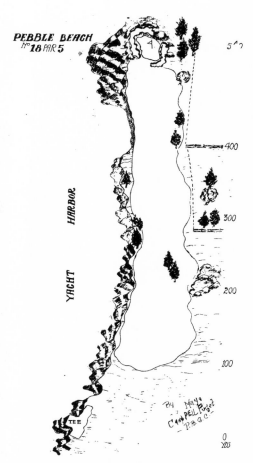

Drawing of the "New" 18th at Pebble Beach Golf Links, Pebble Beach, California, Par-5, 530 Yards

"The tee has been extended oceanward by bridging it over to a nearby rock, thus adding much to its charm. The new green built on the old location is more closely trapped than the old one and now offers a rather difficult target for anything but a short third."

— *H. Chandler Egan*

187

Eighteenth Green at Pebble Beach Golf Links, Pebble Beach, California, Par-5, 530 Yards

The finishing green at Pebble Beach soon after Egan's 1928 remodel. The large bunker fronting the green has since been broken down into two bunkers and the green has been reduced significantly in size.

CHAPTER SEVEN

OTHER SCHOOLS OF DESIGN

Several significant architects practiced during the Golden Age who did not evolve out of any particular school. And some, due to a lack of documentation caused by the Depression, could not receive their own chapter in this book. This is not to downplay the significance of a Perry Maxwell or Stanley Thompson, it is just a matter of fact that their work was not as well documented as an Alister MacKenzie or an A.W. Tillinghast.

Included here in the "Other Schools of Design" are several important architects, as well as a brief look at other designers who were not as well known but who left us with some interesting examples of Golden Age architecture. Perry Maxwell, William Langford, Stanley Thompson, Herbert Strong, Norman MacBeth, William Diddle and Wilfred Reid left several fine examples of architecture that still exist, as well as others which fell victim to the hardships of the Depression or World War II.

PERRY MAXWELL

(*1879-1952*)

A successful banker who took up golf at the age of thirty, Perry Maxwell became one of America's most important, and yet least known architects. His resume is impressive, with two Midwestern mainstays in Southern Hills and Prairie Dunes, not to mention major redesign work at Augusta National, Colonial, Pine Valley, and The National Golf Links.

Maxwell was one of the first architects to promote the practicality of grass greens in the Midwest, and in later years would be best known for the brilliant contouring of his greens. "Maxwell greens," believed to be inspired by the Old Course, could best be described as large with bold swales and quirky rolls, adding interest to some of the less interesting sites Maxwell frequently worked on.

Some of Maxwell's creativity may have stemmed from a brief but successful collaboration with Alister MacKenzie in Michigan. Maxwell oversaw construction at the University of Michigan Golf Club and at MacKenzie's brilliant Crystal Downs, where the two giants of architecture crafted some of the boldest green contours imaginable.

In 1946, Maxwell's right leg was amputated but he continued to take on design projects, with his son Press overseeing the on-site work. He is buried at Dornick Hills Golf Course in Oklahoma, one of his more daring design efforts.

Original Seventh at Prairie Dunes Country Club, Hutchison, Kansas, Par-3, 160 Yards

Playing today as the tenth hole, this is admired as one of golf's best par-3s. Nine holes were added at Prairie Dunes to Perry Maxwell's original design in 1957 by his son, Press. Perry Maxwell spent one month surveying the terrain for Prairie Dunes before settling on an 18-hole routing, though only nine holes were completed when the course opened in 1937.

"It is my theory that nature must precede the architect, in the laying out of links. It is futile to attempt the transformation of wholly inadequate acres into an adequate course. Invariably the result is the inauguration of an earthquake. The site of a golf course should be there, not brought there . . . Many an acre of magnificent land has been utterly destroyed by the steam shovel, throwing up its billows of earth, biting out traps and bunkers, transposing landmarks that are contemporaries of Genesis."

— Perry Maxwell

Eighteenth Hole at Southern Hills Country Club, Tulsa, Oklahoma, Par-4, 460 Yards

One of golf's most famous finishing holes, designed by Perry Maxwell.

192

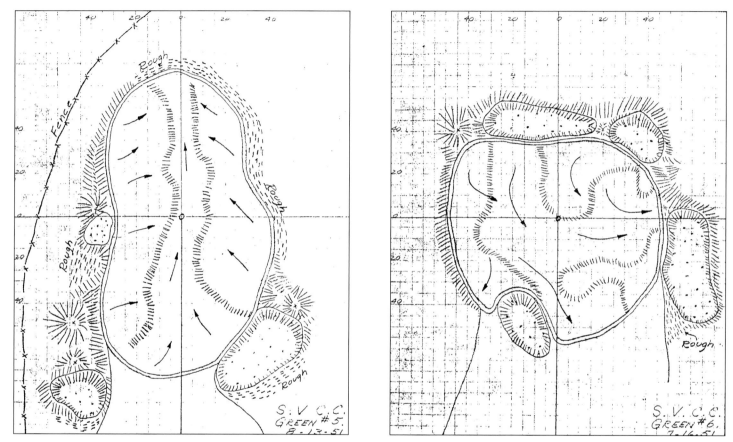

Perry Maxwell Green Renderings, Saucon Valley Country Club, Bethlehem, Pennsylvania
Maxwell was frequently consulted in the 1930s and 40s by some of America's finest clubs to modify or completely redo greens. Here are two drawings by Maxwell for greens to be reconstructed at Saucon Valley Country Club in Pennsylvania (originally designed by Herbert Strong in 1922).

"...the majority of American golf clubs are in the red, gore of the stream shovel, blood drawn by mound builders. We have learned nothing from Scotland and England where the ancient and honorable game can be enjoyed on marvelous links at one-tenth the admission fees, dues, green fees, etc., that prevail in the land of the free."
— *Perry Maxwell*

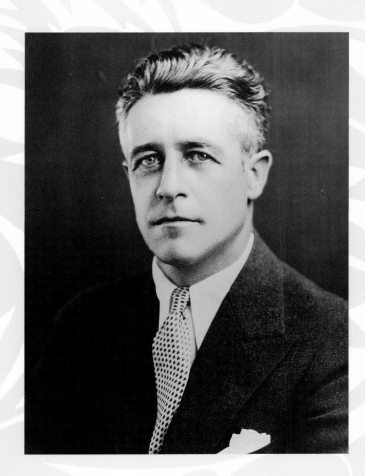

WILLIAM LANGFORD (1887-1977)

William Langford played on three NCAA Championship teams at Yale and reached the semifinals of the U.S. Amateur. He was an outstanding designer of courses throughout the Midwest. Educated as an engineer, he formed his own design firm in 1918 with civil engineer Theodore Moreau.

Like many of his counterparts during the 1920s and '30s, Langford was a strategic designer who emphasized the short game with his undulating greens and deep, grass-faced bunkering. He designed or remodeled some 250 courses during his career. Later on, he even made adjustments to some of his own courses because of changes in equipment and fears that his courses would become obsolete.

Langford's design at Wakonda Club in Iowa and Lawsonia Links in Wisconsin are among his most acclaimed efforts. Langford wrote several fine essays, focusing his thoughts on construction and methods to create more cost-effective designs while maintaining enough interest to build a fine course.

193

194

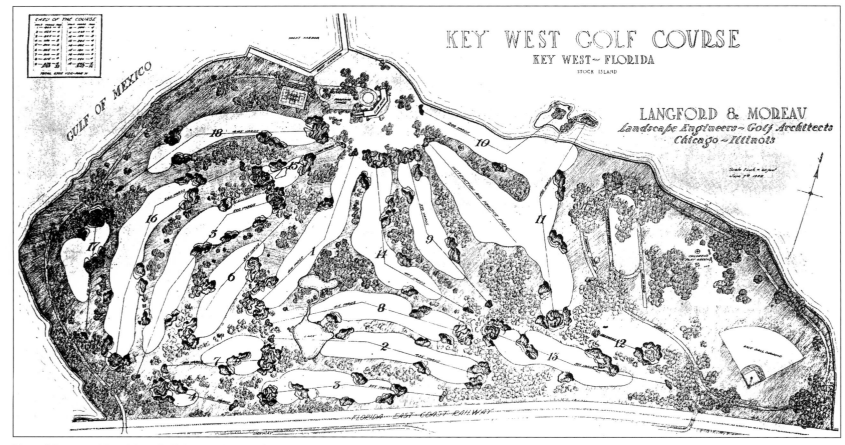

Map of Proposed Key West Golf Course by Langford and Moreau
Note the island green and tee (upper right) Langford and Moreau proposed building for the tenth and eleventh holes at Key West Golf Course in Florida.

Fourteenth Green at Lawsonia Links, Green Lake, Wisconsin, Par-3, 175 Yards
One of the few historic photographs of William Langford's work shows an extraordinarily deep greenside bunker.

"Hazards should not be built solely with the idea of penalizing bad play, but with the object of encouraging thoughtful golf and of rewarding the player who possesses the ability to play a variety of strokes with each club."
— William Langford

Langford Drawings
William Langford was fascinated by alternate-route holes, and here are two examples of his more interesting ideas.

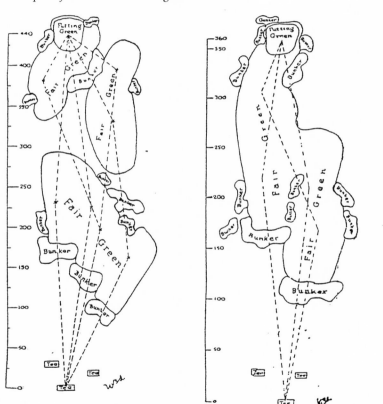

195

HERBERT STRONG (1879-1944)

Once the golf professional at St. George's in England, Herbert Strong moved to Rye, New York in 1905 to become the professional at Apawamis Club. He changed jobs and it was at his new workplace, Inwood Golf Club, that Strong would oversee the complete remodeling of the course in preparation for the 1921 PGA Championship and a U.S. Open two years later.

Based on the strength of Inwood, Strong left the club pro industry to focus his attention on architecture, and his work was best exemplified at three American gems: Engineers Golf Club on Long Island, Saucon Valley's Country Club's Old Course in Bethlehem, Pennsylvania, and Canterbury Golf Club near Cleveland, Ohio. Herbert Strong believed in deep bunkers and bold green contours and although major changes have taken place, his work is still faintly evident today. Strong was also one of the more eccentric early designers, building cavernous bunkers, large sandy "waste" areas, and severe green complexes.

Like many other Golden Age architects, Strong was forced to abandon the design field during the Depression. He returned to other aspects of the golf business until his death in 1944.

Fourteenth Hole at Engineers Club, Roslyn, New York, Par-3, 90 Yards
A rare photograph of the famous "2 or 20" hole, named so because both Bobby Jones and Gene Sarazen went for double figures here. The green is surrounded by a severe natural fall off on three sides, making recovery shots nearly impossible.

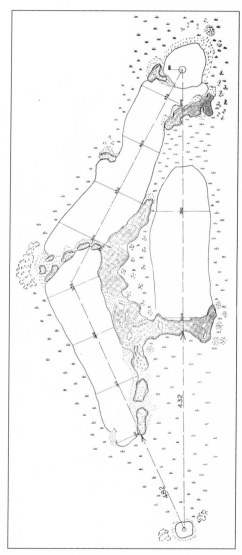

Herbert Strong Green at Lake Forest Country Club, Hudson, Ohio
One of Herbert Strong's boldly undulating greens at Lake Forest.

Drawing of a multiple-option shot hole by Herbert Strong and George Low.

198

STANLEY THOMPSON
(1894-1952)

Canadian Stanley Thompson was an artistic genius who trained many fine architects while churning out an impressive list of courses during the 1920s and '30s. Best known for his early work at the breathtaking Banff Springs Hotel course and at Jasper Park Golf Club in Alberta, Thompson was a fine tournament player who believed that the strategic school was the only true form of golf course design. As with so many other Golden Age architects, Thompson's background as a fine player translated into more credibility as a practicing designer.

Stanley Thompson was one of the first architects to set up a large design firm, employing a soil chemist, plant pathologists, landscape architects, an arborist, and a land planner. With so many experts on the payroll, Thompson focused on his love for designing holes. He was known to spend countless days examining a site before settling on a routing, and he was one of the first to employ many features that would become commonly accepted golf course traits, such as three sets of tees and multiple routes to each hole. He also created intricate models for his crews to work off of in the field.

Besides his two courses in Alberta, Thompson's St. George's in Ontario, Canada and the Ladies Golf Club of Toronto stand out as his best examples of strategic design. Among the future architects who would train under Thompson were Geoffrey Cornish, Robert Moote, Howard Watson, Norman Woods and Robert Trent Jones, Sr.

Sixth Hole at Banff Springs Hotel Golf Course, Alberta, Canada, Par-3, 178 Yards
Stanley Thompson's sixth at Banff provides one of the most dramatic views in all of golf.

Fifteenth Green at Jasper Park, Alberta, Canada, Par-3, 138 Yards
A dramatic one-shotter with a green perched on a small ridge.

Wilfred Reid

A fine player who competed with Vardon, Ray, Jones, Hagen, and Sarazen, Wilfred Reid brought his Scottish influence to the United States and designed several fine courses. Although he served as the pro at such great clubs as Seminole and Indianwood, Reid's most lasting contribution to golf was in the form of architecture. He laid out the original Lakeside Country Club course that would become the Olympic Club, and created one of the best-kept secrets in America to this day, the Old Course at Indianwood. With touches of some of his favorites such as Cruden Bay, Lahinch, and St. Andrews, Indianwood is a rare links style course in the otherwise tree-lined countryside outside of Detroit. Reid incorporated every conceivable natural feature and built a striking variety of greens, including one 10,000 square feet in size.

Twelfth Hole at Kenwood Country Club, Cincinnati, Ohio, Par-3, 160 Yards
William Diddle won several Indiana State Amateur titles before turning to golf course design in the 1920s. He was one of the Golden Age's more fascinating innovators, having built one course (Woodland Country Club, Indiana) with no bunkering and only ground contours to serve as the design features. He also created a "short" ball that would have gone half the distance of a regular ball, presumably to create full-length courses on less acreage. Diddle was also a charter member of the American Society of Golf Course Architects. The twelfth at Kenwood shows some very innovative and artistic bunkering.

Seventh Green and Eighth Hole (left) at Indianwood Country Club, Lake Orion, Michigan
Wilfred Reid's most dramatic design was at Indianwood, which until a recent restoration and the hosting of two U.S. Women's Opens had been somewhat forgotten by the golf world.

Norman MacBeth

A fine amateur player who grew up at Lytham and St. Anne's in England, Norman MacBeth moved to Los Angeles in 1908 and created a successful cement company. MacBeth's love for golf helped him to become a major figure in Southern California golf. MacBeth designed courses on the side, largely to help promote the game in his newfound home. Although Wilshire Country Club in the heart of Los Angeles was his best work, he also created several fine holes at Redlands Country Club in California, where he recruited Alister MacKenzie to help with the design.

Third Green at Indianwood Country Club, Lake Orion, Michigan, Par-3, 170 Yards

Fifth Hole at Wilshire Country Club, Los Angeles, California, Par-3, 170 Yards
Norman MacBeth was one of the first architects in California to incorporate the many native barrancas and arroyos into golf course design. At Wilshire, he built this alternate green one-shotter, which provided two very distinct holes.

Eighteenth Hole at Wilshire Country Club, Los Angeles, California, Par-4, 440 Yards
"Norman MacBeth's course, Wilshire, has some interesting holes. The 18th is magnificent. It has not a single bunker, but owes its excellence to a large deep arroyo running diagonally almost the full length of the hole."

— *Alister MacKenzie*

ABOUT the PAINTINGS

The landscape paintings preceding each chapter were painted specifically for this book with the intent of bringing various Golden Age courses to life, something black and white photography can never completely accomplish. Each work is listed here by title and location, along with the original painting dimensions and commentary on the subject matter.

Paintings by Mike Miller

Cover Painting
After the Rain at Merion
34 3/4 x 24, Oil on panel
The short par-3 thirteenth at Merion plays to a small green surrounded by the unique bunkering found only at Merion Golf Club's East Course. Hugh Wilson designed Merion with help from William Flynn and Joe Valentine.

Title Page
Late Autumn at Los Angeles Country Club, circa 1928
24 x 26 Oil on Panel
The long par-3 eleventh on the North Course, redesigned by George Thomas and Billy Bell in late 1927. The 230-yard hole plays downhill to a raised green fronted by a grouping of impressive bunkers.

Chapter 1—The Early Influences, p. 14
Overview, Second Hole at Royal County Down
24 x 36, Oil on panel
Old Tom Morris is responsible for the character of this remarkable course, located on some of Northern Ireland's finest linksland. Old Tom Morris was the single most influential early architect and perhaps the first professional designer of golf courses.

Chapter 2—The National School of Design, p. 30
Late Summer Afternoon at Fisher's Island
36 x 40 1/4, Oil on panel
Depicted here is Seth Raynor's "Short" hole at Fisher's Island Golf Club, the fourteenth. Raynor studied under National School of Design "founder" and father of American golf, Charles Blair Macdonald.

Chapter 3—The Philadelphia School of Design, p. 50

The Sandy Carry on Pine Valley's Third

36 x 48, Oil on panel

The long one-shot third at Pine Valley is one of the most daunting holes in golf. This view depicts George Crump's expert par-3 in the early 1930s when the pines have begun to mature.

Chapter 4—The Ross School of Design, p. 116

Windy Day at Dornoch

36 x 48, Oil on panel

Donald Ross was most influenced by Dornoch Golf Club's course as a young man. He served as the club's pro and greenkeeper before moving to America, where he incorporated many of its features in his nearly four hundred designs. This is the par-3 sixth, a simple looking one-shotter with a great deal of trouble awaiting the players who lose their tee shot long and to the steep drop off on the right.

Chapter 5—The MacKenzie School of Design, p. 136

Setting Sun at Pasatiempo

36 x 48, Oil on panel

The par-3 eighteenth on Dr. Alister MacKenzie's design at Pasatiempo Golf Club, Santa Cruz, California, featured remarkable bunkering that "bleeds" into the canyon. Doctor MacKenzie lived on the sixth hole at Pasatiempo where he resided for the last three years of his life until his passing in 1934.

Chapter 6—The Monterey School of Design, p. 170

Sunrise at Pebble Beach

24 x 36, Oil on panel

A side view of the seventeenth green at Pebble Beach, circa 1929. The hourglass shaped putting surface is surrounded by what architect H. Chandler Egan called "imitation sand dunes." The artificial dunes were created during Egan's 1928 renovation of the course.

Chapter 7—Other Schools of Design, p. 188

Onset of Fall at Crystal Downs

36 x 48, Oil on panel

A side view of the par-4 eighteenth at Perry Maxwell and Alister MacKenzie's co-design in Northern Michigan, Crystal Downs Country Club.

PHOTO CREDITS & INDEX

207

210

THE GOLDEN AGE of GOLF DESIGN FAMILY TREE

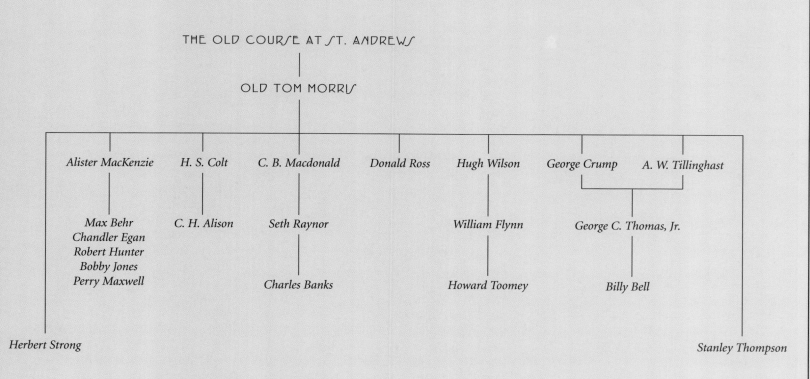

THE OLD COURSE AT ST. ANDREWS

OLD TOM MORRIS

Alister MacKenzie · H. S. Colt · C. B. Macdonald · Donald Ross · Hugh Wilson · George Crump · A. W. Tillinghast

Max Behr
Chandler Egan
Robert Hunter
Bobby Jones
Perry Maxwell · C. H. Alison · Seth Raynor · William Flynn · George C. Thomas, Jr.

Charles Banks · Howard Toomey · Billy Bell

Herbert Strong

Stanley Thompson